STREET SMARTS

High Probability Short-Term Trading Strategies

Laurence A. Connors   and   Linda Bradford Raschke

M. GORDON PUBLISHING GROUP
Los Angeles, California

Copyright © 1995, Laurence A. Connors and Linda Bradford Raschke

ALL RIGHTS RESERVED. No part of this publication may be reproduced, stored in a retrieval system, or transmitted, in any form or by any means, electronic, mechanical, photocopying, recording, or otherwise, without the prior written permission of the publisher and the authors.

Intellectual property rights of the research in this book are owned either by LBRGroup, located at 2 North Country Lakes Drive, Marlton, New Jersey 08053 or Connors, Bassett & Associates, located at 6243 Tapia Drive, Malibu, California 90265.

This publication is designed to provide accurate and authoritative information in regard to the subject matter covered. It is sold with the understanding that the authors and the publisher are not engaged in rendering legal, accounting, or other professional service.

Authorization to photocopy items for internal or personal use, or in the internal or personal use of specific clients, is granted by M. Gordon Publishing Group, Inc., provided that the U.S. $7.00 per page fee is paid directly to M. Gordon Publishing Group, Inc., 1-800-797-2584.

ISBN 978-0-9650461-0-7

Printed in the United States of America

In memory of my grandfather, Manuel Gordon,
who passed away during the writing of this book.
—L.C.

To my husband, Skip, and my daughter, Erika—
the two most special people in my world.
—L.B.R.

Disclaimer

It should not be assumed that the methods, techniques, or indicators presented in this book will be profitable or that they will not result in losses. Past results are not necessarily indicative of future results. Examples in this book are for educational purposes only. This is not a solicitation of any order to buy or sell.

The NFA requires us to state that "HYPOTHETICAL OR SIMULATED PERFORMANCE RESULTS HAVE CERTAIN INHERENT LIMITATIONS. UNLIKE AN ACTUAL PERFORMANCE RECORD, SIMULATED RESULTS DO NOT REPRESENT ACTUAL TRADING. ALSO, SINCE THE TRADES HAVE NOT ACTUALLY BEEN EXECUTED, THE RESULTS MAY HAVE UNDER-OR-OVER COMPENSATED FOR THE IMPACT, IF ANY, OF CERTAIN MARKET FACTORS, SUCH AS LACK OF LIQUIDITY. SIMULATED TRADING PROGRAMS IN GENERAL ARE ALSO SUBJECT TO THE FACT THAT THEY ARE DESIGNED WITH THE BENEFIT OF HINDSIGHT. NO REPRESENTATION IS BEING MADE THAT ANY ACCOUNT WILL OR IS LIKELY TO ACHIEVE PROFITS OF LOSSES SIMILAR TO THOSE SHOWN.

CONTENTS

ACKNOWLEDGMENTS		xi
PREFACE		xiii
Chapter 1	INTRODUCTION	1
Chapter 2	SWING TRADING	5
Chapter 3	MONEY MANAGEMENT	11

PART ONE	TESTS	
Chapter 4	TURTLE SOUP™	21
Chapter 5	TURTLE SOUP PLUS ONE™	33
Chapter 6	80-20's™	45
Chapter 7	MOMENTUM PINBALL™	51
Chapter 8	2-PERIOD ROC	59

PART TWO	RETRACEMENTS	
Chapter 9	THE "ANTI"™	69
Chapter 10	THE HOLY GRAIL	79
Chapter 11	ADX GAPPER	87

PART THREE	CLIMAX PATTERNS	
Chapter 12	WHIPLASH	99
Chapter 13	THREE-DAY UNFILLED GAP REVERSALS	103
Chapter 14	A PICTURE'S WORTH A THOUSAND WORDS	109
Chapter 15	WOLFE WAVES	121
Chapter 16	NEWS	131
Chapter 17	MORNING NEWS REVERSALS	135
Chapter 18	BIG PICTURE NEWS REVERSALS	141

PART FOUR	BREAKOUT MODE	
Chapter 19	RANGE CONTRACTION	151
Chapter 20	HISTORICAL VOLATILITY MEETS TOBY CRABEL	161

PART FIVE	MARKET MUSINGS	
Chapter 21	SMART MONEY INDICATORS	173

Chapter 22	MORE WORDS ON TRADE MANAGEMENT	183
Chapter 23	BE PREPARED!	187
Chapter 24	FINAL THOUGHTS	193
Chapter 25	THE SECRETS OF SUCCESSFUL TRADING	195

APPENDIX 203

Historical Volatility Calculations, 203
Moore Research Center—Statistical Studies, 205

- Exhibit A.1 Historical Upper 90% Statistics, 208
- Exhibit A.2 Historical Upper 80% Statistics, 209
- Exhibit A.3 Historical Lower 10% Statistics, 210
- Exhibit A.4 Historical Lower 20% Statistics, 211
- Exhibit A.5 Historical WR7 and Higher Close Statistics, 212
- Exhibit A.6 Historical WR7 and Lower Close Statistics, 213
- Exhibit A.7 Historical ROCRSI Buy Report, 215
- Exhibit A.8 Historical ROCRSI Sell Report, 216
- Exhibit A.9 Historical Fresh ROC Buy Report, 218
- Exhibit A.10 Historical Fresh ROC Sell Report, 219
- Exhibit A.11 Futures 14-Period ADX Statistics, 221
- Exhibit A.12 Historical Oops Buy Report, 223
- Exhibit A.13 Historical Oops Sell Report, 224
- Exhibit A.14 Historical Oops (ADX Gapper) Buy Report, 225
- Exhibit A.15 Historical Oops (ADX Gapper) Sell Report, 226
- Exhibit A.16 Historical Fresh ADX Buy Report, 228
- Exhibit A.17 Historical Fresh ADX Sell Report, 229
- Exhibit A.18 Historical Gap Failure Buy 50% Report, 231
- Exhibit A.19 Historical Gap Failure Sell 50% Report, 231
- Exhibit A.20 Historical Channel (2-Period High/Low) Report), 233

Samples of Daily Worksheets, 234
Trademarks, 236
Research Services, Software, and Charting Services, 237
Software and Books Offered by Oceanview Financial Research, 238

ABOUT THE AUTHORS 239

ACKNOWLEDGMENTS

This manual could not have been written without the thoughtful assistance of the following friends:

Nelson Freeburg of Formula Research; Tom Bierovic of Synergy Futures; Mark Boucher of Investment Research Associates; Derek Gipson and Sara Shroyer—Who were kind enough to take time out from their busy schedules to give us their much appreciated insights and suggestions.

Toby Crabel, Bob Pearlman and Bill Wolfe—For allowing us to share their trading ideas.

Fernando Diz of Syracuse University—For allowing us to release his research in this manual.

Judy Brown, Danilo Torres, Dan Chesler, Rick Genett, and Elyce Warzeski and associates—For assisting us with the layout and design.

Steve Moore and Nick Colley at the Moore Research Center—For accommodating our time demands to bring us the best testing in the business.

Aspen Research Group, Ltd.—For their superior charting software. All charts in this manual are courtesy of Aspen Research.

Karen Connors—For "enduring with a smile" her husband during the writing of this manual and Brittany and Alexandra Connors who hopefully still remember their father's face.

Bill Masciarelli—The unsung hero of this work.

PREFACE

Traders talk amongst themselves, not necessarily to discuss bullish or bearish market opinions, but rather to share insights into the nature and quirkiness of this business. The mental toll trading exacts definitely forms bonds. When we open up it is always surprising to discover the similarity of lessons learned, experiences shared, and how we all independently arrive at the same conclusions. Often in talking with each other we're really looking for clues into our own heads, hoping to understand ourselves a little better.

Despite our constant pursuit of knowledge, the market itself assures there is no shortcut to obtaining our final degree. In the end, it is experience which is our ultimate teacher and there is no substitute. We can only choose the attitude with which we approach this process of learning to trade. We can accept the inevitable setbacks and learn from them, or we can yield to our natural human stubbornness and be forced to repeat the same lessons over and over again.

This book has been written by two people who have come to enjoy the process. We've both discovered we are not the only ones to have made certain mistakes and we've also discovered the same secrets to success . . . which we hope to share with you. **The single most important secret is this: learn to listen to the markets and do not impose your own will upon them.**

Every successful trader we have known has also discovered the necessity for **consistency**. It is the key to everything—you must trade with a coherent methodology. You must follow a specific trading strategy. Although this book presents multiple strategies, each and every one has the same essential starting point: minimizing risk first, looking to maximize gains only after risk has been defined and controlled.

Between us we have 34 years of experience as floor traders, exchange members, traders on institutional desks, hedge fund managers, and commodity trading advisors—trading for our own accounts the entire time. We hit it off well because our number one guiding belief is that you must, above all, find setups and entries which minimize exposure. The profits come on their own terms.

Finally, even though we present many different patterns, you only need ONE strategy to be prosperous. Some of the best traders are successful because they trade only one strategy. Hopefully, all of the patterns in the manual will increase your awareness of certain market idiosyncrasies and will serve as a confirmation of your own market observations.

CHAPTER 1

INTRODUCTION

Yes, Virginia, you CAN make a living from trading!

In a day when global money managers are given increasing attention and funds seem to dominate the market arena, it might be difficult to imagine that the small speculator could have much of an edge. Has trading become a function of computer power? Have markets changed in the last decade? How relevant is the theoretical world in the heat of battle? The truth is, a few trading tricks and a little common sense will get you more mileage than all the books on technical analysis combined. Ultimately, an individual can better determine support and resistance than a computer can. And yes, the private individual has more of an edge than he knows!

This book is written for the active trader. It is a compilation of strategies that the two of us have been trading with for the last 15 years in both equities and futures. The strategies are conceptually simple and have been readily adopted by our friends and colleagues. This is not a book of technical analysis. It is a manual of precise setups that have you in the market for only a limited amount of time. Consider it to be a collection of "surgical strikes" with a distinct methodology for managing each one!

Each pattern identifies a distinct market condition. After all, trading should be done on only the most recognizable and reliable patterns. Most of the setups can be traded on any market and on any time frame.

This manual will teach you everything we know about swing trading. By swing trading we mean monitoring the market for support and resistance levels and actively trading around those areas. Stops are placed just beneath support or above resistance to minimize risk. You will learn to recognize the best setups at these levels and then how to lock in profits when trades are made.

In order for you to get the most out of trading these setups, a few points need to be covered:

- It is important to initially trade a new concept or strategy on paper. Only by seeing a pattern over and over again will you truly feel comfortable with it. You **must** believe in its ability to repeat itself. Don't be surprised if you find yourself actually becoming excited as you see the patterns begin to set up.

- If a pattern does not make sense to you, don't trade it. If you don't have a 100 percent belief in it, you will not be able to overcome losing streaks.

- **All you need is one pattern to make a living!** Learn first to specialize in doing one thing well. We know two traders who do nothing but trade the "anti" pattern from a five-minute S&P chart. Another friend trades only "Three Little Indians" on tick charts. Traders can earn their living by trading any one of the patterns that we present in this book.

- Your biggest enemy in trading is going to be a directional bias, an opinion about market direction . . . whether yours, a broker's or a friend's. Shut it out! Learn to concentrate on the "right-hand side" of the chart—in other words, on the pattern at hand.

- One of the things you will get out of this book is an increased ability to "listen to the market." Even if a chapter does not seem to suit your personal trading style, it should at least heighten your awareness of market action and price behavior at critical points.

- **None of these strategies is designed to be a mechanical system.** Be grateful that they are not! If they were, a large fund would come into the marketplace and exploit the edge. It is estimated that over 90 percent of the large pools in the commodity markets are run on a mechanical basis, systematically attempting to exploit trends. It is very difficult for these funds to move large amounts of money on a short-term time frame. They do not have the luxury of using resting stop-loss orders without risking adverse slippage. They cannot be as nimble as the small speculator can—and herein lies your **edge**.

- This brings us to the most important point. Initial stop loss orders are essential! Each strategy in this book will have you entering a protective stop upon being filled. Stops are necessary for your protection against worst-case scenarios. (Remember, we are trading on probabilities only.) All it takes is getting sloppy once, or experiencing the "frozen rabbit syndrome" in a bad trade, to undo the efforts of the previous 20 trades. **Placing initial protective stops must become a habit that is never broken.** As you will see, in most, if not all of the examples, your stops will risk only a small amount of money.

The patterns in this manual are organized around three distinct swing trading concepts by which support and resistance levels are formed. They are: tests, retracements, and climax reversals. We will elaborate on these ideas in the introductory chapter on swing trading. This will be followed by a chapter on money management.

Chapters included under "test" setups include Turtle Soup, Turtle Soup Plus One, 80-20's, and Momentum Pinball. Retracement patterns include sections on the Anti and two ADX trades. Lastly, different types of climax reversals are discussed. Our favorites range from news-reversal patterns to distinct bar chart setups.

We have also included a chapter by a friend who is a finance professor at Syracuse University. We thought you would be fascinated—as we were—by the summary of his research and findings on the secrets of longevity and profitability of top CTAs.

The appendix includes all applicable back-testing results independently conducted by the Moore Research Center in Eugene, Oregon. These tests are included to illustrate a market's tendency; that an edge does indeed exist. They are not meant to be mechanical systems.

Before we move on to the strategies, let's first discuss the mechanics of swing trading.

CHAPTER 2

SWING TRADING

■ ■

"Speculation, in its truest sense, calls for anticipation."
Richard D. Wyckoff

It is important to understand the basics of swing trading to understand how our strategies work.

Since the days of Charles Dow, traders have written about two distinct methods of trading. The first is playing for the "long pull." This involves trying to determine the underlying value of a market or security through fundamentals. A trade is then held until a revaluation takes place. This is analogous to trend-following strategies which ultimately depend on long-term economic policies or fundamental shifts in supply and demand. The second method of trading, as described by Dow back in 1908, was to "deal in active markets making many trades, and relying on stop loss orders for protection." This came to be called "swing trading." Trading opportunities presented themselves on both the long and short side, regardless of what the underlying long-term trend was.

Swing trading is anticipating the market's next move, and asking what is the most probable outcome. For example, if a market broke support and had a sharp move down, the strongest trade to make would be to sell the first rally. This is because the most probable event would be for the market to at least make a retest of the new low before it could, with any high degree of probability, be expected to reverse direction again.

The main goal of each trade is to minimize risk rather than maximize profit. Positions are managed according to the market's behavior after we've made our trade. We can't really predict the outcome. For example, if we are trading on a test, we don't know if it will lead to a true reversal or just a consolidation pattern before further continuation of the preceding move. We are trying to achieve a "headstart" in the right direction together with a chance to put in a tight stop.

Trend following gives a trade room to breathe and allows for drawdowns. Swing trading depends on NOT riding out reactions or giving up profits already won. Trades should be exited either in the direction of price movement or just as the price reverses. Trailing stops will lock in any profits gained.

Trading should take advantage of extremes in price action, high volume, and liquidity. All the patterns in this book are designed to capture profits in active market conditions. We will teach you to seek out emotional extremes in the marketplace, and then show how to identify the difference between smart money and late-public buying/selling.

The strongest pattern in swing trading is trading on tests of previous highs or lows. These tests form a "double stop point," and offer an excellent trade entry location with the least risk of loss. A low test at which to

EXHIBIT 2.1 "Double Stop Point"

go long can make either a slightly higher or lower low, but support cannot be established until there has been a test! It is after a successful test (that is, the market has tested a previous high or low and stopped there again), that many of our setup patterns occur.

The second type of trade is made by entering on a reaction or retracement. This is "buying a higher low" in a sequence of higher lows and higher highs (or selling a lower high in a series of lower lows and lower highs). In this case there will only be a single stop point, but since the trade is entered in the direction of the prevailing trend, no test should be required.

EXHIBIT 2.2 "Single Stop Point" in a Trend

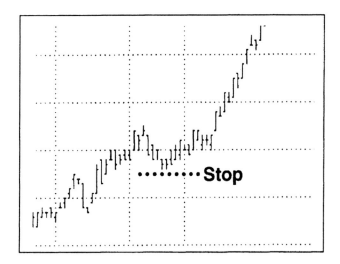

The final type of trade is a climax or exhaustion pattern.

The most successful climax trades will occur in a high volatility environment, and AFTER the market has already reversed. You must see the "climax stop point" already in place before you enter your position! If your entry is correct, the market should move favorably almost immediately.

Swing trading is also learning to ANTICIPATE one of these three types of plays. With the majority of patterns in this book, resting orders can be placed ahead of time, so it is not necessary to watch every tick. However, over time, you should find that your tape reading skill (your ability to follow the market's action) has become greatly refined!

EXHIBIT 2.3 "Climax Stop Point"

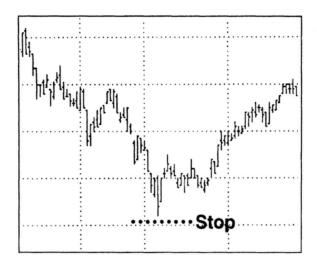

Here are some of the other basic tenets of swing trading:

- Stay in one time frame! Yes, it is important to be aware of the big picture, but it should not affect where you get into or out of a trade or how you manage it. Don't turn short-term scalps into "big picture" trades.

- When in doubt, get out! If the market goes dull and quiet after you enter a trade and makes no progress in the direction of your entry, do not wait until your stop is hit. Just get out! Seek a more active market or better trading opportunity. All of the strategies in this book should reward you immediately. If they don't, it is likely your trade will turn into a losing one.

- Don't trade in quiet, dull markets. Dow, Livermore, Rhea, Taylor, Gann—all the greats say this over and over. There must be activity and liquidity in order to trade profitably.

- **Don't carry losing positions overnight.** Exit and try entering at a more favorable level the next day.

- If the market offers you a windfall profit on a trade, **lock it in!** (*Windfall* means a much bigger profit than anticipated.) Take profits on half or all of the position. Trail an extremely tight stop on any balance!

- Finally, remember that both in short-term trading and mechanical systems, the distribution of winners is skewed. Most of a month's profits might come from only two or three big trades. Much of the time the individual profits may seem small, but more importantly the losses should be small, too.

It is vitally important to "lock in" the best trades. Be defensive and don't give back profits when swing trading!

CHAPTER 3

MONEY MANAGEMENT

"Take every gain without showing remorse about missed profits, because an eel may escape sooner than you think."

Joseph de la Vega, 1688,
in an early manual on trading.

Every trading strategy in this manual is absolutely 100 percent useless without proper money management. We can tell you story after story of very talented traders who blew up because of one or two bad trades. It happened to both of us early in our careers! In our opinion, the overwhelming reason that traders win or lose is not because of their entry method, but because of their money management skills.

By "money management" we simply mean keeping losses and drawdowns to an absolute minimum while making the most of opportunities for profit.

As important as money management is to all investors, it is even more important to short-term traders. Unlike long-term trend followers, short-term traders rarely make a large sum of money on any one trade. Therefore, unlike the trend follower who tolerates a large drawdown in exchange for the possibility of hitting a home run, the short-term trader

11

must keep his losses to a minimum to ensure his survival. **If you keep your losses to a minimum on every trade, you will have 80 percent of the battle won.**

All of the patterns in this book follow the same method of money management. The following principles will ensure your success in **any** type of short-term trading!

1. Enter the entire position at once! This means that if you trade in multiple contracts, put on the whole position at the same time. Do not add to winning positions.

2. Place an initial protective stop on the entire position one or two ticks below the most recent high or low. (The market should **not** come back to this defined support/resistance level, or "risk point!") The exact timing to exit a trade is a subjective matter. What is not subjective is the initial protective stop.

3. Immediately look to scale out of your trade as the market moves in your direction. By taking some of the trade off, you are decreasing your risk and locking in profits. If you are trading on a one-contract basis, as you should if you are a beginner, move your resting stop to protect any gains.

4. **Important**—if the market starts to move parabolically or has a range-expansion move, take profits on the entire position. This is very likely a climax!

A range-expansion move is a very large trading bar caused by the last of the market's participants (the emotional latecomers) dog piling into the market. When this last group of traders has entered, there is nobody left to come in to continue to drive prices up or down.

EXHIBIT 3.1 Range Expansion Move

LARRY:

When I learned to tighten my stops on parabolic moves, I became a more profitable trader. At those times I want the market to take me out before I give back my profits.

LINDA:

When I'm fortunate in catching that type of move, I want to get out in the direction of the trade. That way I at least have the potential for positive slippage. I know there is liquidity, and there are other people willing to take the trade off my hands.

LARRY:

The point is that we are both actively looking to get OUT of the trade and take profits, not looking to add!

LINDA:

Sometimes what happens with a great winning trade is that it feels so good to be in it that we stop thinking about where to take profits. Instead we're thinking, how come I didn't put on a bigger position? This, of course, is most likely the perfect time to be exiting. A friend of mine who has been a professional trader for 20 years has a wonderful saying: "When the ducks quack, feed them." In other words, when everybody wants something, that's probably the perfect spot to sell it to them. The price has already been bid way up. Emotions drive the markets to extremes, and these extremes are the ideal spot to exit our trades.

LARRY:

No matter how long you trade, you'll never do it perfectly. Case in point—A friend of mine is a retired market wizard. This man has made over $100 million trading futures. He told me that his biggest weakness was that he never mastered his exit strategy!

This trader might have been unhappy about the few times he got out too soon, but obviously it was the right way to trade judging from his profits! Maybe there is no such thing as the perfect exit strategy, but you have to lock in profits when they're there, even if it means getting stopped out prematurely on a small reaction.

LINDA:

People tend to focus on the one out of 20 times they really did leave money on the table and not look at all the other trades where getting out was the right thing to do.

The only thing you should look at is how much a winning trade added to your bottom line. This is exactly the mindset of successful floor traders!

Ultimately, the way to minimize risk is to be in the market the shortest amount of time. The longer you are in the market, the more exposure you have to "price shocks" or unexpected adverse moves. As the markets get noisier and noisier, there are more frequent reactions. If you don't take your profits when you have them the market will usually take them back.

You must also learn to do your own thinking and have self-reliance. If you ever have to ask someone else's opinion on a trade, you shouldn't be in it.

LARRY:

I learned that very lesson in 1987. I became very sick with a mental illness known as "Guru-itis." This affliction occurs when a normal, somewhat intelligent individual loses all sense of his abilities and becomes subservient to someone he believes is of greater power. In my case, I became a willing follower of a market guru who had accurately predicted the bull market move of 1984–1987. In late August 1987, with the Dow at all-time highs (2700 range), my guru told his disciples that a grand-supercycle move would bring the Dow up another 700–800 points in a short time.

Up until that point in my life, I had been fairly conservative in my personal finances and was lucky enough to have accumulated a comfortable amount of money. After my guru made his pronouncement via a newsletter, I immediately took a piece of paper and began plotting my course to riches. I divided 800 points (the expected grand-supercycle move) by 8 (the approximate amount of Dow points needed to move the OEX index up or down one point) and came up with the number 100. I then quickly multiplied 100 times $100 (the amount of money one OEX option increases in value on a per point move) and came up with $10,000.

Then I really became excited. If my guru's predictions came true, I would make $10,000 for every OEX contract I owned. The next day I did what every good disciple should do. I began aggressively buying OEX calls. September calls, October calls, multiple strike price calls—you name it, I bought it. Within a few days, nearly 30 percent of my net worth was in these calls. I remember being so excited at the amount of money I was going to make that I could not sleep at night.

Coincidentally, at that time, my wife (who was five months pregnant with our first child) and I had scheduled a two-week vacation on the island of Maui. The morning we boarded the plane the market was up about 15 points, just as my guru said it would be. The six-hour flight was the longest flight in my life. I couldn't wait to land to find out how many thousands of dollars (tens or hundreds?) I had made that day. When we arrived at our hotel, I called my secretary to get the good news. The conversation went something like this:

ME:

Carmel, was the market up 50 points today or did it go up 100?

CARMEL:

(silence)

ME:

Come on, Carmel, give me the good news.

CARMEL:

Down 52 for the day, Larry.

ME:

Sure, Carmel. No really . . . how much did it go up?

CARMEL:

Larry, I'm not kidding.

ME:

Quote me the prices on my options, Carmel.

CARMEL:

(She quotes the prices of the options).

ME:

Sh_t!

I mumbled good-bye to my secretary and immediately called my guru's hotline, "Not to worry," said the main man. "The grand-supercycle high predicted for the near future is still intact." Even though I had taken a beating for the day, I began my vacation assured that riches were just around the corner.

The next day, my wife and I spent the morning looking at condos in Maui. I figured every 28-year-old, soon-to-be-millionaire trader should own at least one. By the time we had finished our house hunting expedition, the markets were closed for the day, and I called my secretary again for the quotes.

CARMEL:

I have good news and bad news.

ME:

Give me the bad news.

CARMEL:

The market lost another nine points today.

ME:

What the hell is the good news?

CARMEL:

It was down more than 35 points earlier.

This time, I didn't mumble anything. I immediately hung up the phone and called the guru's hotline. Once again, he assured us that the grand supercycle was still intact. (I believe psychiatrists refer to this as "denial.") To make a long story short, this scenario took place day after day. What should have been a very relaxing vacation turned into 14 days of misery. (We all know what happened to the market shortly thereafter.)

The message from us is this: do not let your decisions be swayed by the predictions of gurus and experts. By following your own counsel and only trading the strategies that you are comfortable with will you be able to avoid situations like the above story and maximize your abilities as a trader.

PART ONE

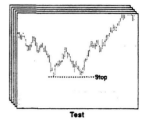

TESTS

CHAPTER 4

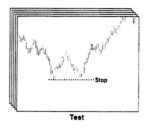

TURTLE SOUP™

The Turtle Soup[1] pattern typifies the basic testing concept in swing trading. It is a volatile pattern with the potential for substantial gains. It is initially not as easy to trade as it looks, but the reversals that follow through indicate a potential change in trend of significant duration, and a very tight risk point is predefined.

Before looking at the rules for this pattern, let's talk about its background. In the 1980s, a group of traders known as the Turtles used a system that basically employed a 20-day breakout of prices. A four-week price breakout was also earlier popularized by Richard Donchian as a standard trend-following strategy. If prices made a new 20-day high, one would **buy**; if prices made a new 20-day low, one would **sell**. It tends to work in the long run if traded on a large basket of markets because there are high odds that something unusual will occur in a market somewhere, such as a Persian Gulf War (crude oil), or a freeze (coffee). The system is very dependent on capturing an extraordinary event or significant trend. However, it also tends to have very large drawdowns and a low win-loss ratio due to the significant number of false breakouts. This is where the Turtle Soup opportunity lies!

---

[1] The name of this strategy should not be construed as disrespect for the Turtles or anyone trading the turtle system. Some friends humorously called this pattern Turtle Soup, and the name has stuck.

Our method is to identify those times when a breakout is false and to climb aboard for the reversal. Many times, when the market is trending strongly, the false breakouts will be short lived. However, a handful of times the reversals are intermediate- to long-term trend reversals that lead to spectacular gains.

Like every other strategy presented in this manual, this is not a mechanical system. The trade must be managed according to the money management rules outlined in the preceding chapter. Due to the liveliness of the market action around these 20-day high and low points, you should watch for them to set up so as to anticipate the volatility and subsequent trading opportunity.

Here are the rules:

FOR BUYS (SELLS ARE REVERSED)

1. Today must make a new 20-day low—the lower the better.

2. The previous 20-day low must have occurred at least four trading sessions earlier. **This is very important**.

3. After the market falls below the prior 20-day low, place an entry buy stop 5–10 ticks above the previous 20-day low. This buy stop is good for today only.

4. If the buy stop is filled, immediately place an initial good-till-canceled sell stop-loss one tick under today's low.

5. As the position becomes profitable, use a trailing stop to prevent giving back profits. Some of these trades will last two to three hours and some will last a few days. Due to the volatility and the noise at these 20-day high and low points, each market behaves differently.

6. *Reentry Rule:* If you are stopped out on either day one or day two of the trade, you may reenter on a buy stop at your original entry price level (day one and day two only). By doing this, you should increase your profitability by a small amount.

Let's look at a handful of examples from 1995.

EXHIBIT 4.1 S&P—December 1995

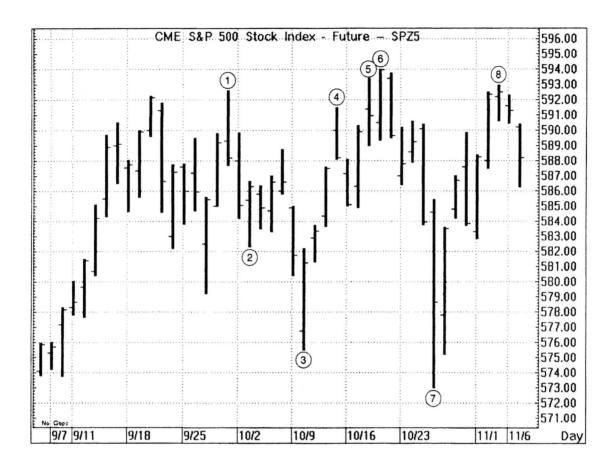

1. On September 29, the market makes a new 20-period high and reverses. The previous 20-day high was 592.25, made on September 20, which is at least four previous trading sessions from today. We go short at *592.00*, five ticks under the September 20 high. Our initial protective stop is placed at 592.65, one tick above today's high.

2. The market trades to as low as 582.00 two days later. A trailing stop assures us of locking in a large portion of the profits.

3. October 10, a 20-period low and a reversal. The previous 20-day low was made on September 27 at 579.20. Our buy stop placed five ticks above the September 27 low is filled and we are long. An initial protective sell stop is placed at 575.45, one tick below today's low. As the position becomes profitable, we will of course, move our stop up quickly.

4. The market rallies sharply over the next few trading sessions, taking the index to above the 591 level, 12 points above our entry.

5. A losing trade. The market makes a new 20-period high and reverses. We are filled at 592.35, five ticks under the previous 20-day high made on September 29. A protective buy stop is placed one tick above today's high of 593.40.

6. We are stopped out near the close for a loss of 1.05 points (plus slippage and commission).

7. A new 20-day low. The previous low was at least four trading sessions earlier. As the market reverses, we are filled five ticks above the October 10 low. Our sell stop is initially placed one tick below today's low.

8. The market rallies more than 16 points in five trading sessions!

EXHIBIT 4.2 Bonds—September 1995

1. July 7, 1995, bonds make a new 20-period high and reverse. The previous 20-day high was made at least four trading sessions earlier (6/23) at 115–30. We go short in the 115–25 range with a protective stop one tick above today's high of 116–06.

2. Bonds begin a gradual sell-off that leads to a parabolic drop on July 19. As we mentioned in our introduction, whenever this type of extended range move occurs, we tighten our stops since many times such price action signals the end of a move. In this example, bonds drop over five points from our entry point.

EXHIBIT 4.3 Copper—December 1995

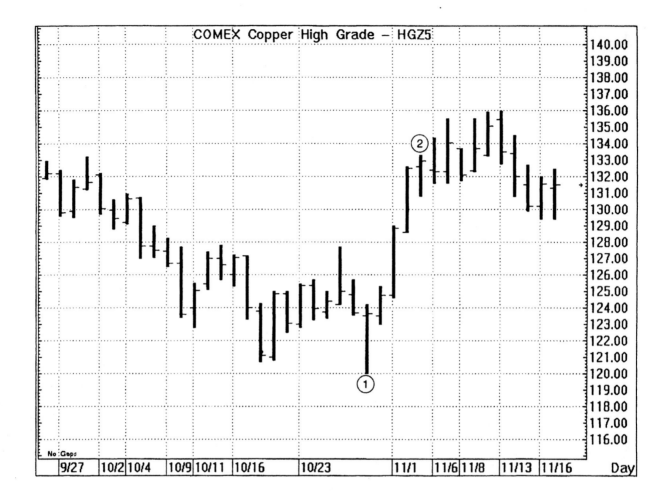

1. October 30, 1995, a new 20-period low and reversal. The previous low was made at least four trading sessions earlier on October 19 at 120.80. We go long in the 121.05 area with a protective stop at 119.95, one tick below today's low.

2. The market rallies more than 10 cents in a week.

EXHIBIT 4.4 Hewlett-Packard (HWP)—1995

1. Hewlett-Packard makes a new 20-period low and reverses. The previous 20-period low was made at least four trading sessions earlier. We go long in the 72 1/2 area. (Please note for equities—we enter a Turtle Soup set-up approximately 1/8 of a point below or above the 20-period high or low.) Our protective sell stop is placed 1/8 of a point under today's low of 71 1/2.

2. Over the next two weeks, HWP rallies more than 15 percent.

EXHIBIT 4.5 Yen—September 1995

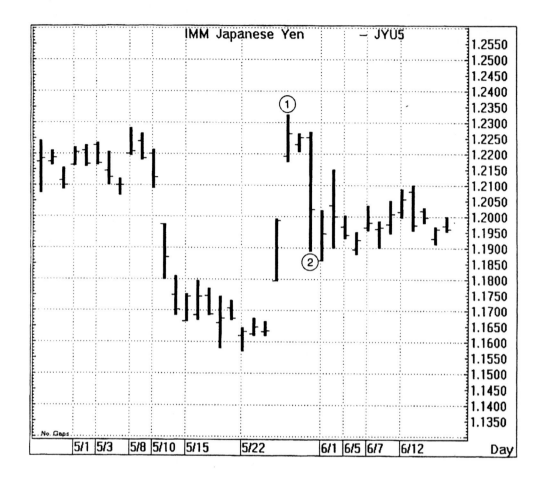

1. A 20-period high. The previous 20-period high was made on May 8, which is at least four trading sessions earlier. After the market makes a new high, it reverses under the May 8 high and we are short. Our protective buy stop is initially placed at 123.26, one tick above today's high.

2. A parabolic drop to under 119. When we see this type of sharp sell-off, we tighten our stops immediately to assure locking in our profit.

EXHIBIT 4.6 Coffee—July 1995

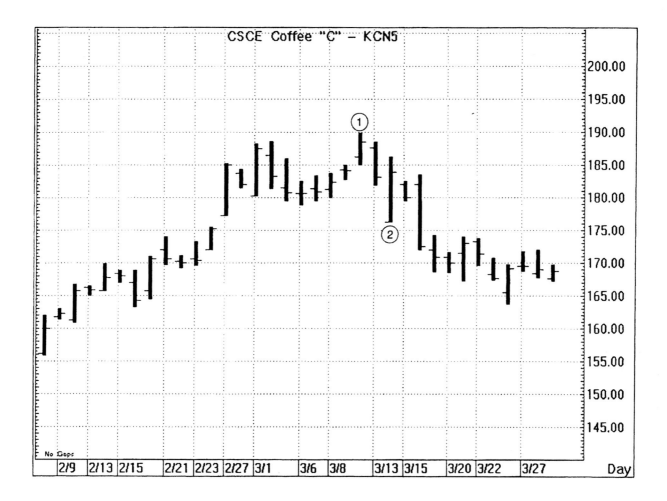

1. The market makes a new 20-period high and reverses. The previous 20-period high is at least four trading sessions earlier.

2. A very sharp sell-off. (Please note that this is where trading this pattern becomes difficult.) On March 14, the market opens approximately 12 points(!) under our fill from two days earlier. As you can see, it immediately rallies sharply higher. It would be imprudent to allow such a large profit to dissipate. Even though the sell-off resumed over the next few days, it is safe to assume we would be out of the position.

EXHIBIT 4.7 Natural Gas—September 1995

1. August 3, 1995, natural gas makes a 20-period low and reverses. Our buy stop is filled in the 1.400 range and our initial protective sell-stop is placed one tick below today's low.

2. The market rallies sharply taking prices to above the 1.570 area within six-trading sessions.

LINDA:

Larry, how did you come up with the Turtle Soup strategy?

LARRY:

It came about over a matter of time. I attempted (unsuccessfully) to trade breakouts of momentum growth stocks as taught by William O'Neill in *Investors Business Daily*. I was frustrated, though, at how many times I got stopped out before a big move occurred. And being a short-term, high percentage trader I didn't enjoy the drawdowns. Also, I had read the Turtles' methodology and learned their system was also plagued by false breakouts.

LINDA:

So, you created a methodology to take advantage of the false breakouts.

LARRY:

That's right. It is a structured method to trade failure tests. One of the drawbacks of this pattern though, is that you will have periods where you can get a large number of 20-day highs/lows that do not reverse. This is time consuming and frustrating. On average, though, about 15–20 trades across 30 futures markets will occur per month. I also look for this pattern on equities.

LINDA:

It appears you're not the only one looking at these points. My office has monitored these levels for years. What do you advise people to do about the volatility?

LARRY:

This strategy requires rigid stop methods. Many times you are entering markets that are going through strong trending periods and after a short correction, the trend continues.

LINDA:

So, you trade this method for only a few days?

LARRY:

Yes, and this is where it gets subjective. This setup has the potential for longer-term, spectacular gains. Because I trade on a short-term horizon, though, I never fully participate in these larger moves. I am comfortable taking a good profit for a few days' work. Those individuals with longer-term time frames may want to look at this setup as one that can occasionally provide them with substantial profits. This can also be done with options, but that is not what I do.

LINDA:

Are you saying then that as your position becomes more profitable over a few days, your stops become tighter and tighter?

LARRY:

Exactly. I am looking to lock in profits whenever possible. I don't look back and concern myself whether or not I missed an eventual big move.

Now let's look at the Turtle Soup Plus One pattern.

CHAPTER 5

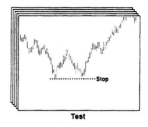

TURTLE SOUP PLUS ONE™

The Turtle Soup Plus One setup is almost identical to the Turtle Soup setup, except it occurs one day later. It too, can be traded in all markets and in all time frames. We are looking for the market to make a new intermediate-term high/low and then reverse the **following** day.

With so many trend-following/breakout players in the investment arena, the rewards are large when a breakout fails and reverses. This is especially true if the market has given players a chance to add on to existing positions. This pattern is also profitable because some players only enter on a **close** outside a new 20-day high/low. Thus, the market has trapped even more participants.

Here are the rules:

FOR BUYS (SELLS ARE REVERSED)

1. The market makes a new 20-day low. The previous 20-bar low must have been made at least three trading sessions earlier. The **close** of the new low (day one) must be at or below the previous 20-bar low.

2. An entry buy stop is placed the next day (day two) at the earlier 20-day low. If you are not filled on day two, the trade is canceled.

3. If filled, place a protective sell stop one tick under the lower of the day-one low or the day-two low.

4. Take partial profits within two to six bars and trail a stop on the balance of your position.

Let's now walk through some examples.

The Turtle Soup Plus One setup identified the 1994 high for bonds.

EXHIBIT 5.1 Bonds—March 1994

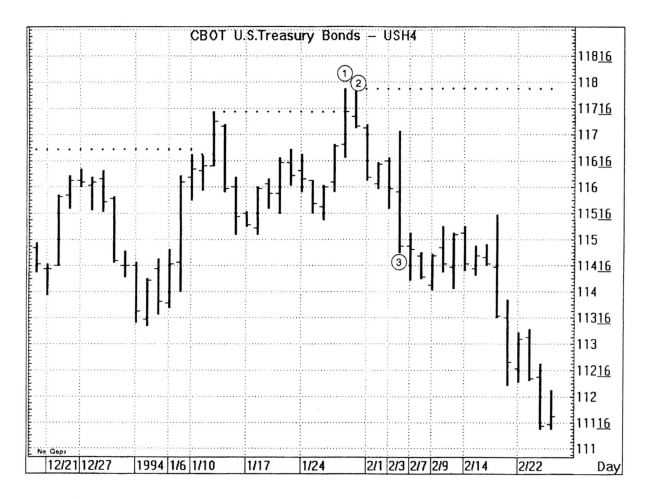

1. March bonds make a 20-period high. If they trade tomorrow under the previous 20-period high made on January 12, we will go short.

2. Bonds open at 117-09 and we are short. We place our initial protective stop at 117-29, one tick above the previous day's high.

3. Like the Turtle Soup strategy, this is where it gets subjective. Bonds have a strong intraday rally and reverse. This reversal takes prices to as low as 111 1/2 over the next two weeks. Because the two of us are short-term traders, we would have locked in our profits on February 4, missing the larger move.

36   Chapter 5

EXHIBIT 5.2 Soybeans—July 1995

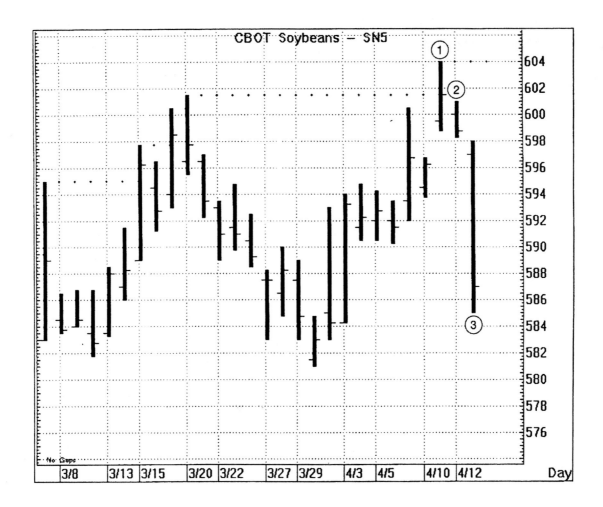

1. April 11, 1995, soybeans close at a new 20-period high. If they trade under the previous 20-period high made March 20, we will look to go short.

2. Soybeans open under the previous 20-period high and we are short. Our protective sell stop is one tick above yesterday's high of 604.

3. The sell-off is significant. Soybeans lose over 25 cents in four trading sessions. Note the sharp sell-off on April 13. After a day like this, you may want to lighten your position or tighten your stops more than usual to take advantage of the move.

EXHIBIT 5.3 S&P 500—December 1994

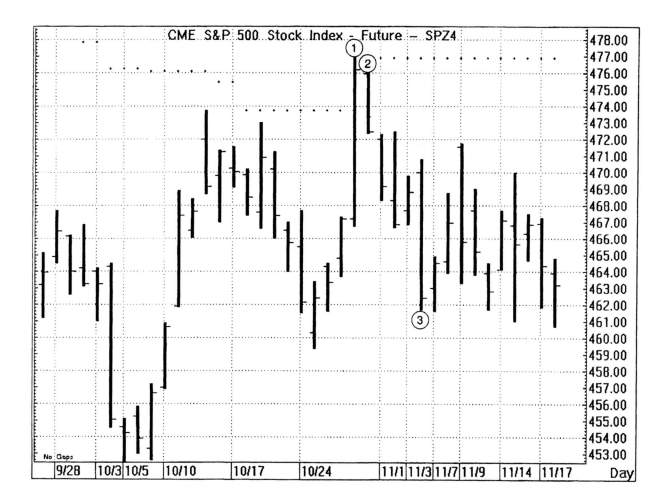

1. New 20-bar high and a close above the previous period's high.
2. A sell stop is placed at 473.75 which is the 20-day high made on 10/13.
3. Four trading days later the market is 12 points lower.

38   Chapter 5

EXHIBIT 5.4   Delta Airlines (DAL)—1995

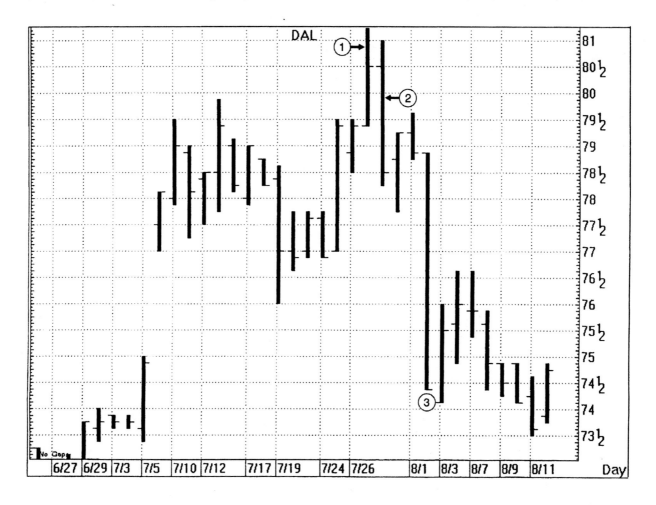

1. New highs (caused by record earnings).
2. Sell short at 79 7/8. Stop at 81 1/4.
3. 5+ points lower in a few days.

EXHIBIT 5.5 Texas Instruments (TXN)—1995

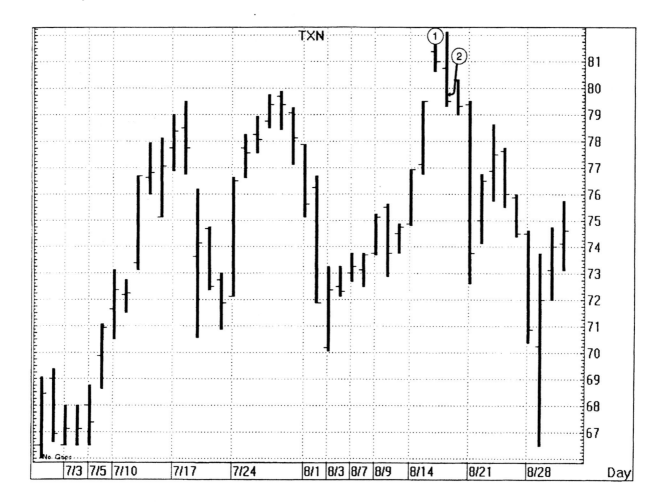

1. 20-bar high.
2. Sell short in the 79 7/8 area.
3. A 14-point gain in nine days.

40   Chapter 5

The Turtle Soup and Turtle Soup Plus One strategies work in all time frames. Here are two examples using 10-minute bars. Please note: When we trade the strategies intraday, we enter at the previous 20-bar high(low) minus(plus) one tick.

EXHIBIT 5.6 Bonds—10-Minute

1. A 20-bar low.

2. The next bar trades above the previous 20-bar low (made in the first 20 minutes of trading).

3. The market rallies 1 1/2 points in less than three hours.

EXHIBIT 5.7 S&P 500—10-Minute

1. A 20-bar high that reverses back into the previous 20-bar high. Sell at 604.75 with a protective stop at 605.15, one tick above the day's high (total risk is .40 points plus slippage and commission).

2. The market closes nearly three points under our entry.

LINDA:

Larry, this strategy obviously evolved from Turtle Soup.

LARRY:

Yes, when I started researching Turtle Soup, I noticed that a good percentage of the reversals occurred one day after the 20-day high/low.

LINDA:

Why do you think that happens?

LARRY:

I can only guess that the second day gets the last of the momentum players in. If they are the last players to buy or sell, the reversals become even greater.

LINDA:

That means more players need to liquidate their positions if they are wrong.

LARRY:

Yes. Also, I like this setup because it is easier to monitor than Turtle Soup. As you can see from the examples in the Turtle Soup chapter, some of the 20-day highs/lows were made with no warning. With Turtle Soup Plus One you know the evening before if a setup exists.

LINDA:

It's easier to do your homework at night.

LARRY:

That's right. However, as with the Turtle Soup strategy, the one drawback is the number of times you will identify markets making 20-bar highs/lows that do not reverse the next day.

LINDA:

Do you trail your stops as aggressively as with Turtle Soup?

LARRY:

Yes, the volatility is just as great, and I want to ensure myself of locking in profits whenever they exist.

The Turtle Soup setups are two of the most exciting patterns we trade. By identifying these setups, you are potentially putting yourself in the position to participate in some very significant reversals. Even if you do not trade this strategy on a regular basis, we highly recommend you at least make a habit of monitoring these 20-period levels.

CHAPTER 6

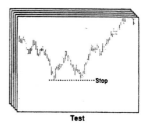

80-20's™

The 80-20's is a strategy we use for day trading. Many of our readers may already be familiar with The Taylor Trading Technique,[1] which is a reference manual for swing trading. Simply stated, Taylor's method implies that markets move with a natural rhythm that is made up of a buy day, sell day, and sell short day. This pattern is further evidenced by the research done at the Moore Research Center by Steve Moore.

Steve profiled days that closed in the top 10 percent of their range for the day. He then tested for the percentage of times the market exceeded the profiled day's high the following day and the percentage of times it actually closed higher. His research showed that when a market closed in the top/bottom 10 percent of its range, it had a 80–90 percent chance of follow-through the next morning but actually **closed** higher/lower only 50 percent of the time. This implies that there is a good chance of a midday reversal.

How could a methodology be created that would profit from this reversal phenomenon? Derek Gipson, a fellow trader, noticed that the market has an even higher likelihood of reversing if the setup bar opened in the opposite end of the daily range, so we added a prequalification that the

---

[1] *The Taylor Trading Technique*, George Douglass Taylor.

market must open in the lower 20 percent of its daily range. Then to create more trading opportunities, we dropped the closing range function down from 90 percent to 80 percent. This did not affect the overall profitability. If the market opened in the lower 20 percent of its daily range and closed in the upper 80 percent of its daily range, a sell setup would be indicated for the next day (and vice versa for buys).

Finally, as with all of the strategies presented, night data are ignored. The range should be created from day-session data only.

Here are the rules:

FOR BUYS (SELLS ARE REVERSED)

1. Yesterday the market opened in the top 20 percent of its daily range and closed in the lower 20 percent of its daily range.

2. Today the market must trade at least 5–15 ticks below yesterday's low. This is a guideline. The exact amount is left to your discretion.

3. An entry buy stop is then placed at yesterday's low.

4. Upon being filled, place an initial protective stop near the low extreme of today. Move the stop up to lock in accrued profits. This trade is a day trade only.

To give you a better feel for this strategy, let's look at a few examples.

EXHIBIT 6.1   Bonds—December 1995—15-Minute

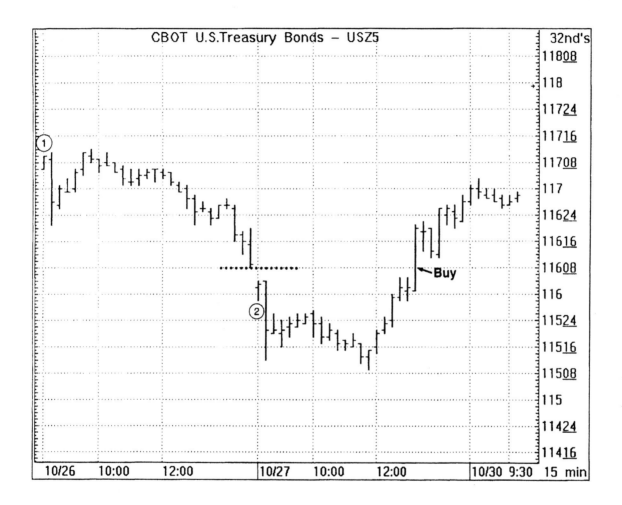

1. October 26, 1995, bonds opened in the upper 20 percent of their range and closed in the bottom 20 percent of their range.

2. Today's bonds trade at least five ticks below yesterday's low and reverse. We go long at 116-08 and the market rallies 3/4 point.

EXHIBIT 6.2 Cotton—December 1995—15-Minute

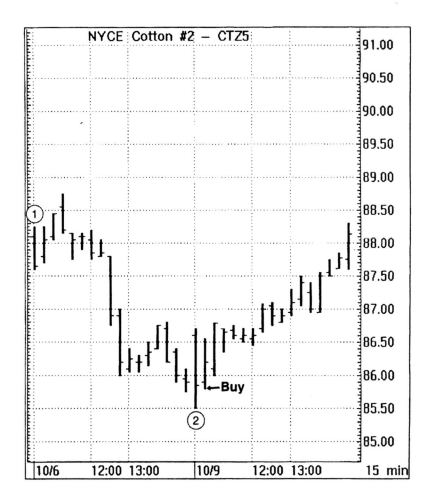

1. October 6, 1995, cotton opens in the top part of its range and closes in the bottom 20 percent.

2. The next day cotton trades at least five ticks below the previous day's low and reverses. We go long at 85.80 with our stop in the 85.50 range. The market proceeds to rise over 200 points by the close. (Remember, this is a scalping strategy that exploits the daily reversal tendency from the previous day's pattern. Large profits from 80-20's are the exception, not the rule.)

EXHIBIT 6.3 Soybeans—January 1996—15-Minute

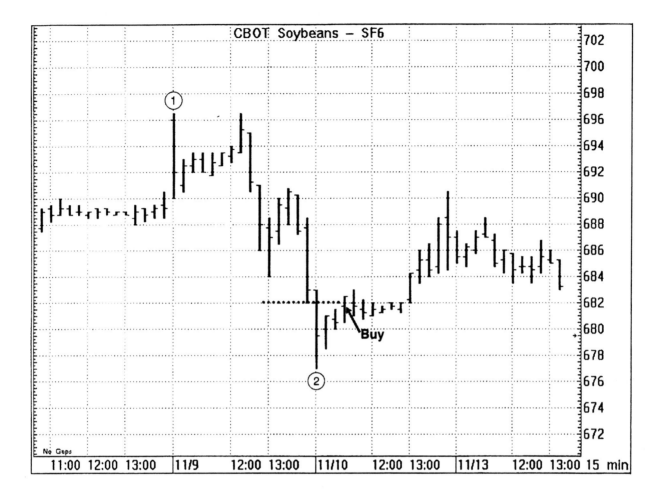

1. On November 9, soybeans open in the top of their range and close near the bottom.

2. The next morning they trade at least five ticks under the previous day's low and reverse. Our buy stop at the previous day's low of 682 is filled. A protective sell stop is placed in the 677 area. Beans trade sideways and then move nearly nine cents higher. A stop is trailed appropriately to capture the gains.

LARRY:

80-20's are low-risk setups for day traders. When the bar following an 80-20 bar takes out the previous day's high/low and then reverses, it represents a failure test of the high or low. This is always one of the strongest places to put a stop. The buying from the previous day has exhausted itself, and the latecomers (weak hands) cannot sustain the move.

LINDA:

This pattern does not necessarily have any long-term implications. It will, though, capture Taylor's market rhythm of one to two day setbacks. It represents a classic short-term swing trade.

LARRY:

Again, this is not a mechanical system. We just want to take advantage of the times the market loses steam and reverses. Another filter one may wish to look at is the size of the setup bar.

LINDA:

That's right. I especially like to look for reversals after bars that have a larger than normal daily range.

LARRY:

With correct money management and stop placement, you can make this a profitable part of your day-trading methodology.

Tables are given in the Appendix that show all of Steve Moore's original research. As you can see, 80-20's capitalize on the market's high tendency for reversal, and this sets up a high probability short-term trade.

CHAPTER 7

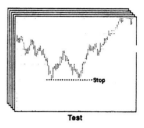

MOMENTUM PINBALL™

One of the most confusing aspects of Taylor's trading technique is knowing whether it's a buy day or a sell short day. Taylor kept a very mechanical book, but even so he made trades which seemed out of sequence. He would actually short on a buying day, except then he would change the name to "buying day high made first!" This is not very helpful to traders trying to learn his technique. The "Momentum Pinball" will automatically tell you if you should be buying or shorting the next day. As with the 80-20's pattern, there is no long-term directional significance to this indicator. However, for short-term (one- to two-day) flips, it can't be beat.

There are lots of tricks one can do with short-term rates of change. This pattern uses a one-period rate of change or "momentum" function. This is simply the difference between today's close and yesterday's close. (i.e., if today's closing price was 592 and yesterday's closing price was 596, the difference is –4.) A three-period RSI of this one-period change is calculated. (Most software charting packages allow the user to do studies on studies in just this way.)

Here are the rules:

BUY SETUP

1. Plot a three-period RSI of a one-period rate of change (the daily net change). We refer to this as an LBR/RSI™.

2. Day one is determined by an LBR/RSI value of less than 30.

3. On day two, place a buy stop above the HIGH of the first hour's trading range.

4. Upon being filled, place a resting sell stop at the low of the first hour's range to protect your trade. The market should not come back to this point.

5. If the trade does get stopped out, it can be reentered on a buy stop at the original price. It is rare that this situation occurs, but when it does it is profitable to reenter the trade.

6. If the trade closes with a profit, carry it overnight.

Exit on morning follow-through the next day (day three). Be sure to exit this trade by the close of the next day. Taylor would look to exit a long trade "just above the high of the previous day."

SELL SETUP

The rules for shorting are the opposite of the buy rules. Day one is determined by an RSI value greater than 70. Place a sell stop below the LOW of the first hour's trading range. A protective stop should always be placed AT the extreme of the bar of entry and then trailed to protect any accrued profits.

The following examples should help clarify this strategy.

EXHIBIT 7.1 S&P—December 1995

1. Yesterday's LBR/RSI close below 30 gave us our first buy signal on the chart. We enter a long position on a breakout of the first hour's range. The trade closes with a profit so we carry it overnight. The next morning the market gaps up and we look to take profits on the trade.

2. On the first sell setup on the chart, we are pulled into a short trade on a penetration of the first hour's low. The market closes on the low for the day so we carry the trade home overnight. The next morning the market gaps lower and we take profits on our short sale.

3. This is another perfect buy example. Notice how many times the market gaps in our favor when we carry a profitable trade home overnight.

4. On this buy example we are pulled into a long trade that does not close as strongly as the first two buy examples. The market closes flat and we carry the trade home overnight. We exit the next day with a small profit. As you can see on points 2 and 4, it is best to exit this trade the following day instead of turning it into a longer-term trade.

5. On this day we had a sell setup from the previous day's reading above 70. However, the market never traded below its first hour's range. Consequently, our sell stop was not hit and no trade was taken.

6. Points 6, 8, and 10, are trades taken from the long side. All trades were profitable and should have been exited the following day.

7. Here is a trade we entered on the short side on a breakout of the first hour's range. The market actually rallied back at the end of the day and our trade closed flat. However, the market still closed below its opening price and we were not stopped out. We hold the position overnight and the market gaps in our favor the next day by over two points.

8. Another sell setup (point 9) but our short entry was not hit. The market did not make a lower low off the first hour's range but instead rallied and closed on its high. This is a perfect example of why we enter on a breakout of the first hour's trading range. We must have confirmation that the market is moving in the direction of our signal to enter this trade.

EXHIBIT 7.2 IBM 1995

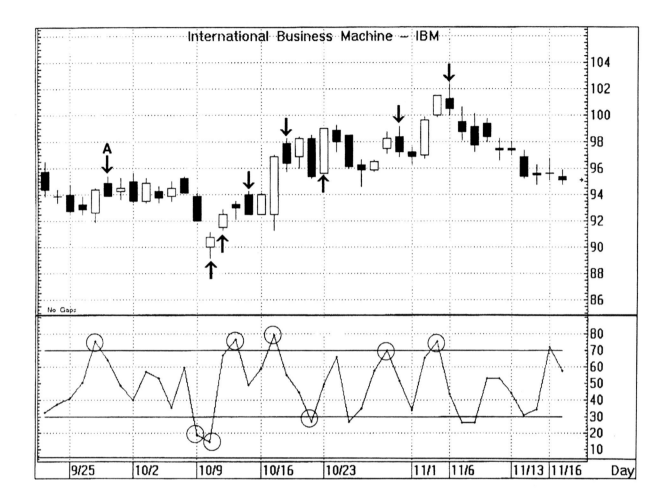

This method works equally well with equities. It is important to select markets with a good average daily range. Otherwise the spread between your entry and exit the following day will be too small, as in point A at the beginning of the chart.

56   Chapter 7

EXHIBIT 7.3 Orange Juice—November 1995

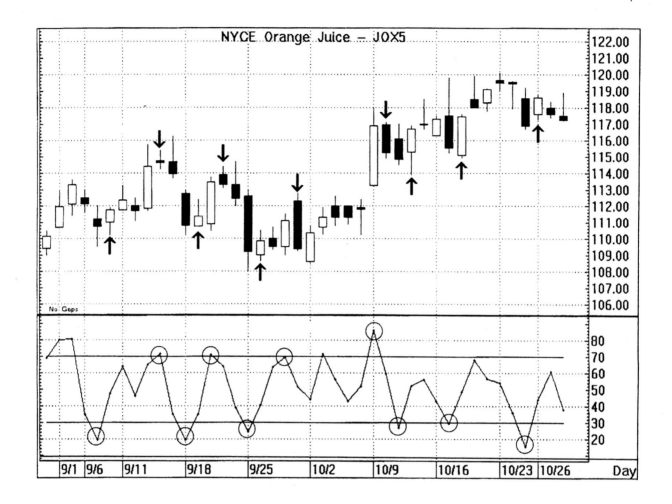

The arrows on this chart show the days where trades would have been taken. Study the examples and note how most of the trades only last one or two days. Do not overstay your welcome using this technique!

Let's look again at the reasons why this trade works so well. First, the day-one setup indicates an exhaustion of buyers/sellers, just as the 80-20's setup does. This is because the momentum indicator functions as a minor overbought/oversold indicator. Second, we are waiting for confirmation that the market is moving in our direction by entering on a first-hour breakout. Quite often the market makes a reversal in the first hour, hits the buy/sell stop, and then moves in our favor for the rest of the day. This reversal tends to be a test of the previous day's high/low.

Over the years we have learned that if a trade closes in our favor, we should hold it overnight. The probabilities favor a bit more follow-through the next day.

LINDA:

This strategy has turned into one of my most consistent trading patterns. Like the Turtle Soup Plus One, it's an easy one to setup the night before.

LARRY:

What's nice about this overall pattern is that you've identified the times the market has become overbought or oversold on a two to three day basis. I've noticed that there's some overlap between this setup and the 80-20's bars, yet they both test out independently and have different entry techniques.

LINDA:

Yes, it's nice to have an overall structure in place instead of putting oneself in a "reactive" mode and getting caught up in too much market noise and crosscurrents. That's usually when you're most likely to get sloppy and forget to put in a resting stop or to hold a marginal trade too many days. "Hope" can be a trader's worst enemy.

LARRY:

You're right. Good habits are everything. Some of these patterns might seem simple, but you must create a methodology for trading them and learn to use trailing stops. Also, it's very important to identify extremes where you have the highest probability of a good reversal.

LINDA:

Lastly, it's important to keep one's profit expectations low. That way you'll be pleasantly surprised when the good reversals occur. It's sort of like fishing. You keep dropping your line in the water, catching little minnows, and once in awhile you will catch a big fish! This is what Momentum Pinball is all about.

CHAPTER 8

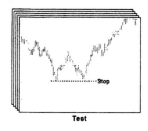

2-PERIOD ROC

This chapter should really be titled "Pinball—Part 2!" Instead of using a one-period rate of change, we are going to use a 2-period rate of change. We will then calculate a short-term pivot point to tell us when the 2-period rate of change is going to flip from a buy to a sell or vice versa. This pivot then tells us whether we want to go home long or short by the close on a fresh signal change. It is best used in conjunction with Taylor's swing trading methodology.

Before we continue, let's review the main principles of Taylor's trading technique.

Taylor observed that the market tended to make a swing high or swing low every two to three days. The market would alternate between this buying pressure and selling pressure, which could then be captured by entering a position on one day and taking it off the next. Thus, a market could be traded back and forth systematically regardless of the overall trend or fundamental outlook. Taylor labeled the days as a "buy" day, "sell" day, or "sell-short" day, and gave each one specific rules for entry.

We are going to concentrate on the rules for a buy day and a sell short day. A buy day sets up after the market has sold off for one to two days. (In a downtrend, the market might need one more additional day to sell off.)

The ideal buy day opens on its low and closes on its high. In the morning, a buy day should find support at the previous day's low. Sometimes it will make a slightly higher low or a lower low, but this **test** (i.e., the low made first on the buy day) is what defines the support level. This then allows us to see our risk point where we can place a protective stop and to enter a long position.

After a buy day entry, we monitor the market to see if it closes higher than its opening. If it does, we will carry the trade home overnight. The market should not make new lows in the afternoon after we bought it. If it does, we will be stopped out since our morning support stop will have been penetrated. If the trade is a winner, we will look to exit the next day. The ideal spot to exit is above the high of our entry day. The trade is trying to take advantage of the tendency for morning follow-through as demonstrated in the test profiles we looked at for the 80-20's days.

On a sell-short day, the market should make its highs first in the morning. The previous day's high is the resistance level that the sell-short day then tests. The sell-short day does not have to exceed the previous day's high; it may make a lower high. If the market makes a morning test of the previous day's high and reverses, we will go short "at the market" and put a stop just above this test point. If the trade closes with a profit, we carry the trade home overnight and look to exit the following day. If it starts to make new highs in the afternoon, our stop will take us out. The market will then probably close higher and it would be better to try shorting the market the next day (hopefully at higher levels) than to carry a losing trade home overnight.

This is the essence of Taylor's trading method. The most important concepts are looking for morning tests (just as in Turtle Soup), and trading off morning reversals (just as the 80-20's bars do). Concentrating on just one entry or exit each day is much easier psychologically than day trading which has the stress of monitoring both the entry and the exit on the same day. Carrying winning trades home overnight is a good habit you should form. What is amazing are the additional profits which can be made playing for the next morning's follow-through.

The biggest obstacle people have in using Taylor's methodology is figuring out which day should be a buying day and which one should be a shorting day. As we've said, Taylor kept a rigid mechanical trading book, but he also had all sorts of quirky rules for shorting on buying days and vice versa. We do not want to get that complicated.

Voila le 2-period rate-of-change! A short-term pivot point can be calculated which will tell us when the 2-period rate of change is going to change direction. We want to be long by the close if the price is trading above this pivot point and short by the close if the price is below this pivot point. We will then look to exit the next day.

This is how you calculate the short-term pivot point for the 2-period rate of change:

1. Subtract today's close from the close two days ago (not yesterday but the day before). Thus, close (day one)—close (day three) equals the 2-period rate of change.

2. Add this number to yesterday's closing price (day two).

3. This will be our short-term pivot number. We want to go home long if we have been on a sell signal and the price then closes above this pivot number. We will look to short if the 2-period rate of change flips from a buy to a sell and the price is going to close below the short-term pivot number.

This is what a worksheet would look like:

Date	Close	2-Period ROC	Short-Term Pivot	Go Home
10–30	586.70			
10–31	583.85			
11–1	588.25	1.55	585.40	long
11–2	592.35	8.50	596.75	long
11–3	592.50	4.25	596.60	**short**
11–6	591.30	–1.05	591.45	short
11–7	588.20	–4.30	587.00	short
11–8	594.10	2.80	591.00	**long**

Let's walk through the calculation. The difference between the close on 11-1 (588.25) and the close two days ago on 10-30 (586.70) was 1.55. This number is added to the close on 10-31 to come up with a short-term pivot of 585.40 which will be used to monitor the close on 11-2. Since the signal was already "long" coming into 11-2, we would only be looking to go short on a close below the pivot. The next day, 11-2, the price closed at 592.35—higher than the pivot—so, we did not go home short. On 11-3, the price closed at 592.50—below the previous day's pivot of 596.60 and a new short signal. Thus we would go home short, looking to exit the next day.

Let's look at some chart examples and observe how this indicator highlights the two to three day market cycles.

EXHIBIT 8.1 S&P—December 1994

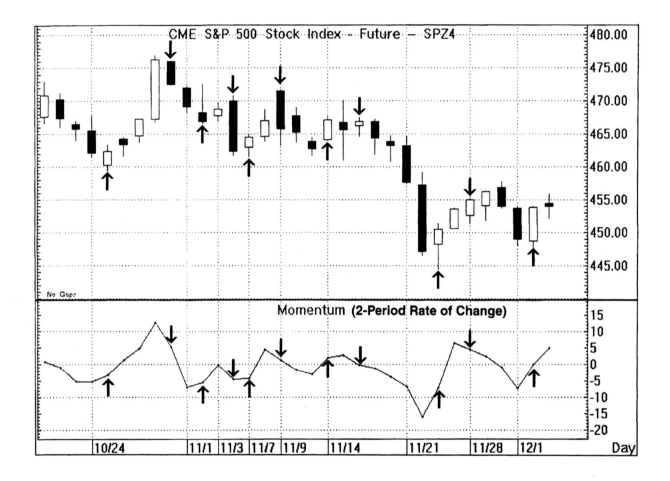

The arrows on the chart show the days where the 2-period rate of change reversed direction. If you had entered on the close of a fresh "flip" and exited on the close the following day, you would have been profitable on 8 out of 11 trades. Although we do not recommend trading this way on a mechanical basis, you can see how this is a useful tool for deciding whether you want to be a buyer or a seller the next day.

EXHIBIT 8.2 Soybeans—November 1995

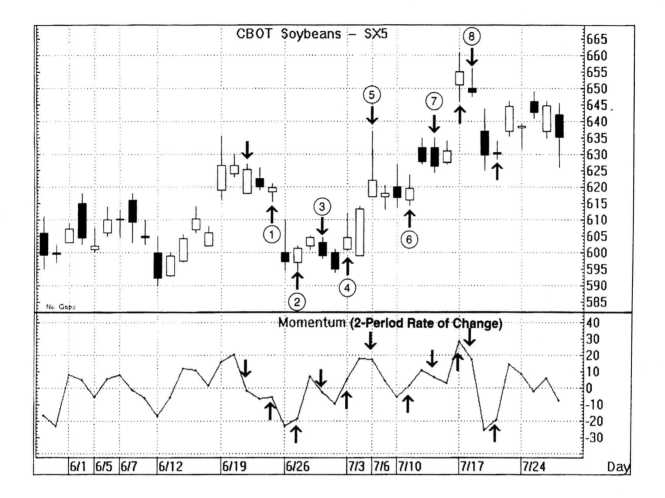

In both discretionary trading and mechanical trading, you will have unavoidable losers (point 1). There will also be small windfalls (point 8). Notice how nicely Taylor's rhythm sets up. Point 2—buy day, exit the next day. Point 3—sell short day, exit the next day. Point 4—buy day, exit the next day. Point 5—sell short day, exit the next day, etc. On balance, this is a winning methodology.

EXHIBIT 8.3 Micron Technologies (MU)—1995

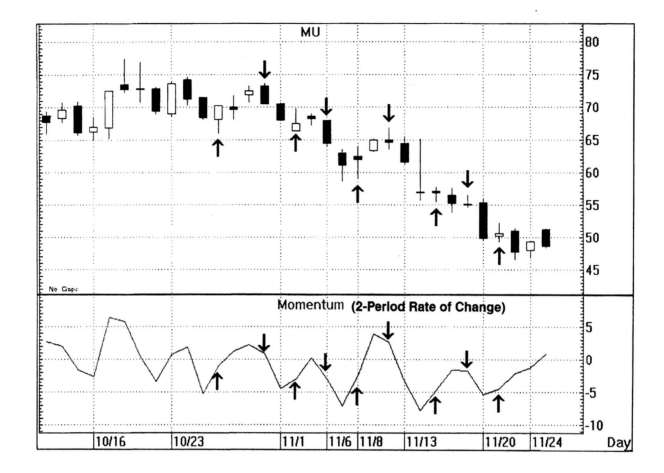

The same three-day cycle also works in equities. Notice that the profits from the buy days are smaller in a downtrend, yet they are still profitable on average. This stock also has a wide daily trading range which makes it a good candidate for active, short-term trading.

LINDA:

I felt that the 2-period rate of change had to be mentioned in this book because I have been trading with it for so long. **I use it in all markets, but I use it only as a guideline.** It is a very noisy oscillator and is prone to whipsaw action at times in flat quiet markets (for example, when the ADX is less than 16). I have spent many years studying it and observing its nuances, and you can do the same. However, I would not recommend that beginning traders pay too much attention to it because it gives many false signals in quiet markets and encourages a trader to make too many marginal trades. It is also not an appropriate tool in a strong-trending market (for example, when the ADX is greater than 30 and still rising.)

Both this indicator and the Momentum Pinball work best in nice choppy markets or **after** a runaway move has already occurred. Learn first to recognize when a market has good volatility and daily range. Then think about applying Taylor's rules in conjunction with the short-term pivot point demonstrated above.

Short-term momentum functions also serve as a departure point for use in mechanical trading systems. The studies presented in the Appendix show that this indicator provides a statistically significant edge. All the tests are run with just one variable. Apply a longer-term trend indicator, a volatility filter, and a money-management algorithm, and you have a fine mechanical trading system!

PART TWO

RETRACEMENTS

CHAPTER 9

THE "ANTI"™

The next four strategies are examples of retracement patterns. They all enter in the direction of a longer-term trend after a pullback in that trend. What's interesting about this next pattern is the way the trend is defined.

The "Anti" pattern is one of the most reliable ways to use an oscillator for spotting and trading a choice swing setup. The trade may not always be apparent on the bar charts alone! Once you understand the principle of the "Anti," it will open up a whole bag of tricks. You can literally spend hours studying this powerful technique.

LINDA:

> I bought my first charting software, INSIGHT, in 1986. I immediately felt like a kid in a candy shop. There were so many technical tools to play with. But soon I was at a loss because tools which I had been using since 1981 were not included in the package. (These were a 3–10 moving-average oscillator with a simple 16-period moving average of itself.) I tinkered with the %K and %D stochastic to try and duplicate the 3–10 oscillator. I found that by using a 7%K and a 10%D the "Anti" pattern worked even better than it did with my old tools.

The basic principle is that a short-term trend will tend to resolve itself in the direction of the longer-term trend. Two different time frames or cycles moving in the same direction create a condition called "positive feedback." This in turn creates some powerful, explosive moves.

For this setup, trend will be defined by the slope of the slow %D stochastic. (The parameters are listed again below.) The first thing you might notice is that often the %D slope is positive while the slope of a moving average is negative (or vice versa). This is because we are really measuring the trend of the momentum. Momentum often precedes price, so it is useful to know when this line is leading or rolling over.

Here are the rules for the setup:

1. Use a seven-period %K stochastic (the "fast" line). If your program allows for an adjustment of the smoothing of this parameter, default to four.

2. Use a 10-period %D stochastic (the "slow" line).

BUY SETUP (SELLS ARE REVERSED)

1. The slow line (%D, the dotted line in the examples on the following pages) has established a definite upward trend.

2. The fast line (%K, the solid line) has begun to rise along with the slow line. A consolidation or retracement in price causes the fast line to pull towards the slow line.

3. Enter when the price action causes the fast line to turn up once again in the direction of the slow line (forming a hook).

TRIGGER

If you are anticipating this setup, there are two easy ways to enter that give you quite a bit of extra edge.

1. When the %K and %D have formed opposing slopes for at least three days, creating a tension between them, place a buy stop one tick above the previous day's bar. (This will be to go long when %D has returned to a positive slope.) If the buy stop is not hit, keep on trailing it down to the high of each previous day's bar.

2. A trend line can also be drawn across the tops of the congestion or retracement pattern. Sometimes this setup captures moves out of small "flags" or "drift" patterns. Other times it captures beautiful moves out of setups that the eye would not normally pick out on a price chart.

LINDA:

I have also entered many times after the "hook" in the fast line has occurred. This is usually a strong enough pattern that it is OK to enter a bit late. The only word of caution is that the average holding time is three to four days. If you get in after the hook has already formed, be prepared to exit within two days.

INITIAL STOP

As with all swing patterns, once the market has turned, it should not look back. The initial stop should be placed just below the bar of entry. It is better to get stopped out and reenter later than to risk too much on the initial trade. By studying the examples and examining this pattern on your own charts, you will quickly see that there is little risk of the good trades getting stopped out.

Once you are in a winning trade, look to exit on a buying or selling climax within three to four bars. This is not a long-term trade, just a quick "Thank-you very much!"

EXHIBIT 9.1 Crude Oil—December 1995

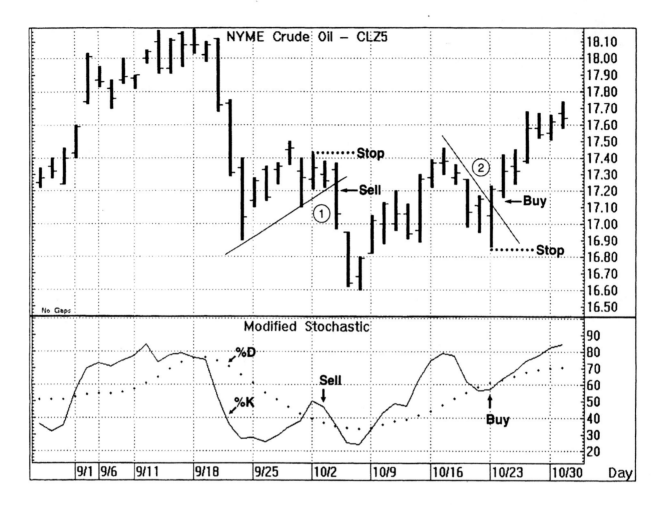

1. The %D has a negative slope. The %K hooks down. We enter a short position on the open the next morning. Our initial stop is entered at the small swing high. The market should not come back to this point. Confirmation of the short sale is given by the break of the trend line containing the consolidation area. The market falls a quick 60 cents in our favor. If you do not take profits on this dramatic drop, a trailing stop should lock in at least half of the gains.

2. A buy setup three weeks later. The %D has a positive slope. The %K hooks up. We enter the trade on the opening the next morning, or if we have been anticipating this set up, we enter the trade on the penetration of the trend line. Our initial stop is placed at the most recent swing low. The market should not come back to this point. We look to exit within two to four bars as that is the average holding time for the "Anti."

EXHIBIT 9.2 Cotton—December 1995

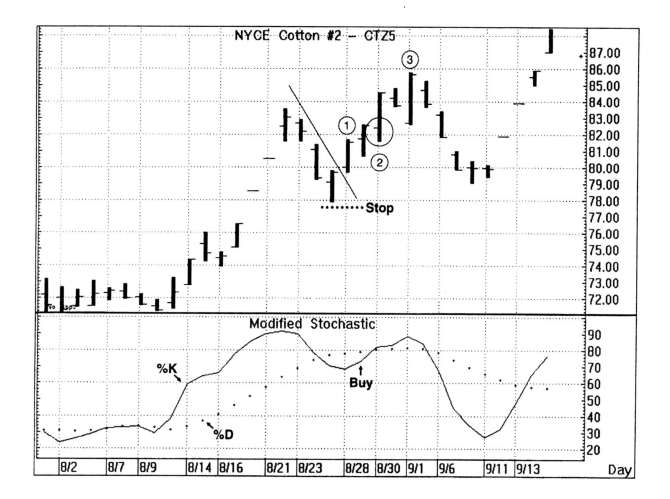

The sharp slope of the %D indicates a good upward trend. The %K pulls back for five days, signaling a correction. Aggressive traders have an opportunity to enter early on the break of the trend line at point 1. Conservative traders can enter on the next day's opening at point 2 after the %K hooks up. Our initial stop is placed beneath the low of the retracement; we should look to exit within two to four days. The market gave us a good range expansion bar at point 3. This would have been the ideal place to take profits.

74 Chapter 9

EXHIBIT 9.3 Micron Technologies (MU)—1995

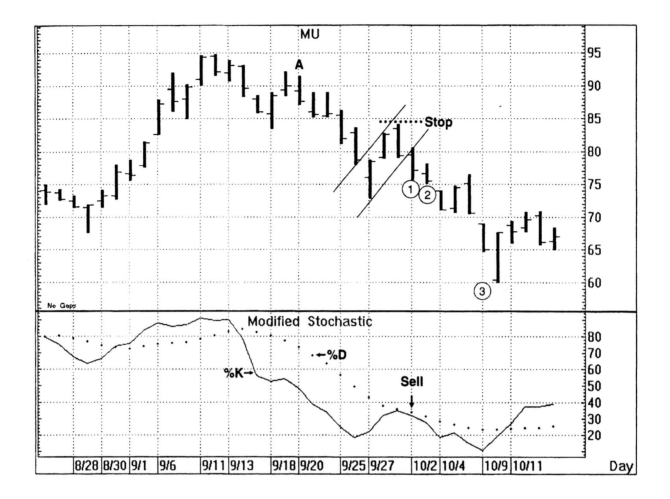

A small drift pattern is highlighted by the retracement in the %K. At point 1, a small trend line is broken and the %K hooks down. We enter the market on the opening the next day. The market was accommodating and provided us with a selling climax on the fourth day at point 3. You will notice a small one day set-up at point A. These occur all the time and are tradable as long as you place an initial stop. However, this pattern is best used to capture breakouts from congestion areas that last two to four days.

EXHIBIT 9.4 S&P—5-Minute

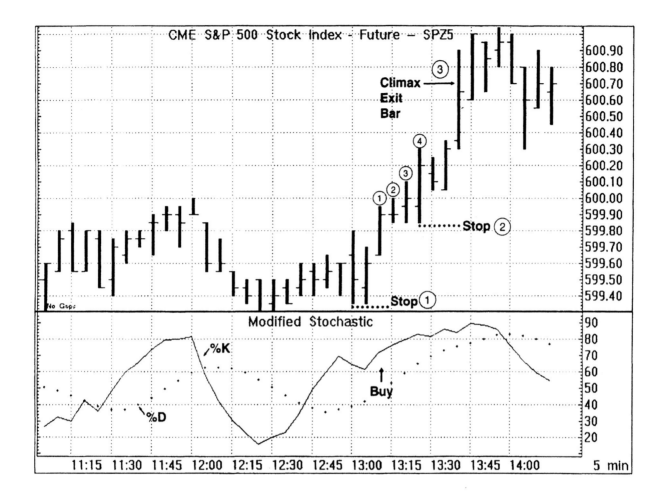

The hook up in the %K signals the breakout from congestion. The momentum (%D) is already trending up. We enter this trade at-the-market and place our stop beneath the swing low at point one. After four bars up, we move our stop up to point 2, the next higher low. The market has met its time objective of two to four bars and there is no guaranty of continuation. At point 3, the market gives us a range expansion bar, the ideal spot to exit this trade.

EXHIBIT 9.5 S&P—5-Minute

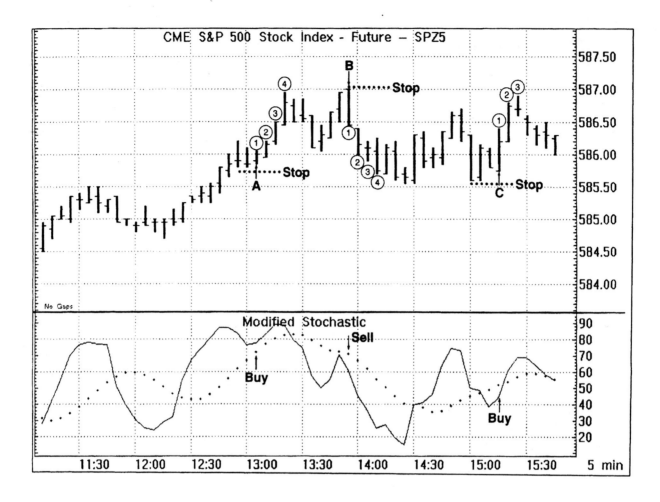

There are three examples on this chart. Each setup occurred after an established trend in the %D, and each had an initial stop point. Learning to place an initial resting stop-loss in the market is always the most important step to trading success. Notice that the majority of time we are in this trade for no more than 10 to 20 minutes (two to four bars.) The less time that we are in the market, the less risk we have. The people who trade this pattern off five-minute S&P charts spend lots of time reviewing their charts at night. This process helps develop a feel for what the "choicest" set-ups look like.

As with any true principle of price behavior, this pattern will work equally well on all time frames, across all equities and futures markets.

LINDA:

I like to use the "Anti" on daily charts, and I have two or three friends who do very well with it on five-minute S&P charts.

LARRY:

What I especially like about the "Anti" is that it does a great job of identifying breakouts from consolidation patterns. It seems to me that many people only use oscillators to identify overbought or oversold situations.

LINDA:

Right! That is also one of the easiest ways to get in trouble if you ignore a strongly trending market. With this setup, the slope of the %D will identify the trend of the momentum. The best trades occur when the %K corrects back at least two to three bars. These are the types of setups which I like to trade because they tend to be the most explosive.

CHAPTER **10**

THE HOLY GRAIL

Just kidding about the title! We named this chapter the Holy Grail because this is one of the easiest patterns in this manual to trade. Based on Welles Wilder's ADX (Average Directional Index) this strategy works in any market in any time frame.

Before we continue, you will need to be familiar with the ADX. Simply stated, the ADX measures the strength of a trend over a period of time. The stronger the trend in either direction, the higher the ADX reading. (If you would like more information about the construction and interpretation of the ADX, we recommend that you read *Technical Traders Guide to Computer Analysis of the Futures Market* by Charles LeBeau and David W. Lucas.)

When prices make new highs(lows) in a strong trend, you should always buy(sell) the first pullback. The Holy Grail is a precise method we use to measure when to enter a position after a retracement. Once we are in this trade, we are looking for a continuation of the previous trend.

One of two outcomes typically follows. The retest will either fail at the previous high/low in which case a small profit can usually be made. In the second scenario, a whole new continuation leg begins. At the very least, one is offered a very low-risk entry point with several options for managing the exit thereafter.

FOR BUYS (SELLS ARE REVERSED)

1. A 14-period ADX must initially be greater than 30 and rising. This will identify a strongly trending market.

2. Look for a retracement in price to the 20-period exponential moving average. Usually the price retracement will be accompanied by a turn-down in the ADX.

3. When the price touches the 20-period exponential moving average, put a buy stop above the high of the previous bar.

4. Once filled, enter a protective sell stop at the newly formed swing low. Trail the stop as profits accrue and look to exit at the most recent swing high. If you think the market may continue its move, you might exit part of the position at the most recent swing high and tighten stops on the balance.

5. If stopped out, reenter this trade by placing a new buy stop at the original entry price.

6. After a successful trade, the ADX must once again turn up above 30 before another retracement to the moving average can be traded.

EXHIBIT 10.1 Wheat—December 1995

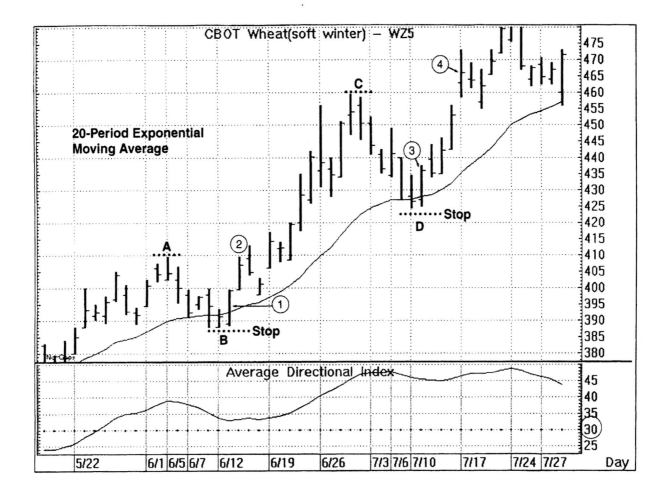

The 14-period ADX is greater than 30 and the price retraces to the 20-period exponential moving average. At point 1 the market breaks out above the high of the previous bar, signaling a long entry. Our initial stop is placed at B, the most recent retracement low. Our trade objective is a test of point A, the most recent swing high, which was met at point 2.

Another trade sets-up in July. The price trades at the 20-period moving average and a buy stop is place above the high of the previous bar. We are filled at point 3 and our initial stop is placed at D, the retracement low. We are anticipating a test of point C, the most recent swing high and this objective is met at point 4.

EXHIBIT 10.2 Citicorp (CCI)—1995

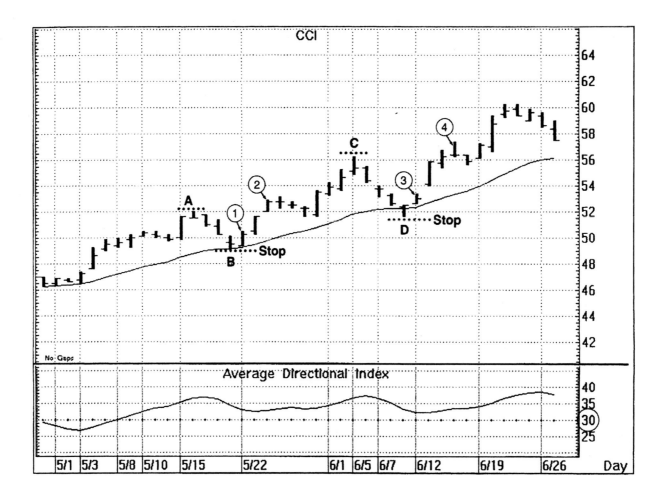

Two trades set-up on this chart. The ADX is greater than 30 and the price corrects back to the 20-period exponential moving average.

Our buy stop is filled above the high of the previous bar. An initial stop is placed at B, the retracement low. We are looking for a retest of point A. Our trade objective is met at point 2. Another trade is entered at point 3. The market reaches our level C objective at point 4.

EXHIBIT 10.3 Russel 2000 Index

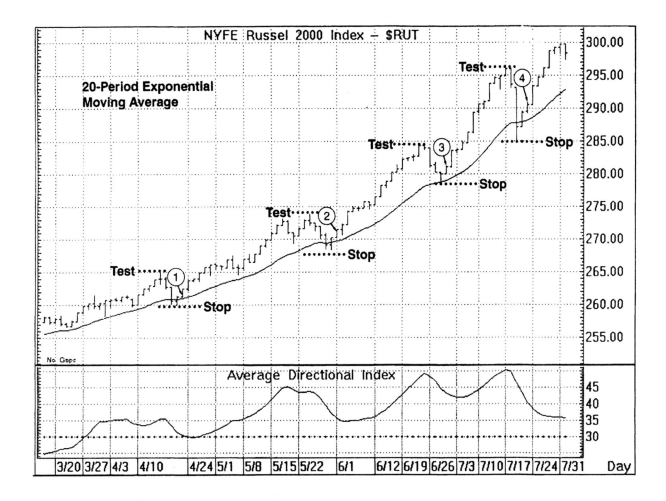

Even if we are not actually trading a market index, this set-up is still useful in our overall market analysis. Four entry opportunities were given in one of the strongest bull markets in the last five years. This example was striking in how well the price was contained by the 20-period exponential moving average.

84   Chapter 10

EXHIBIT 10.4   Orange Juice—60-Minute

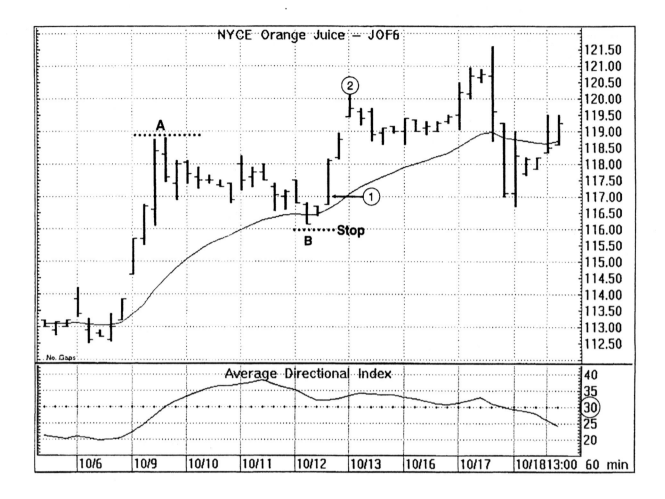

This pattern is particulary well suited for intraday trading. At point B, the market retraces to the 20-period exponential moving average and the ADX is greater than 30. We enter at point 1 on a buy stop above the previous bar's high and begin to anticipate a retest of level A. Our initial stop is placed at B—we are risking no more than $150 on this trade. The market closes in our favor so we carry the trade home overnight. The next morning's follow-through occurs in the form of an opening gap up where we exit our trade.

EXHIBIT 10.5 S&P—60-Minute

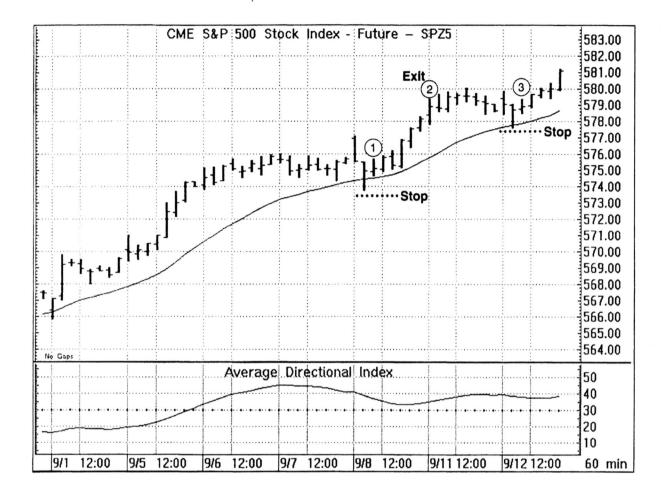

This market was so strong that the price met the 20-period exponential moving average by going sideways for a period of time instead of pulling back. We enter at point 1 where the market takes out the previous bar's high, and then place a stop at the most recent low. The market makes a new leg up and the small range expansion bar at point 2 signals the move is over. A period of rest follows where the market again corrects sideways instead of going down. Another trade could be taken at point 3.

When prices retrace after a strong move, we have found that the 20-period moving average tends to act as support/resistance for these retracements. By waiting for the market to move above the previous day's high, you have more certain confirmation of the resumption of the longer-term trend.

PLEASE NOTE: Many traders have the misconception that a turndown in the ADX indicates a trend reversal. This is rarely true. Usually, the ADX initially peaks as a price consolidation begins. This setup is easy to find. We hope that you will spend time studying the charts and examining it for yourself. We think you'll soon come to see why we named this chapter "The Holy Grail!"

CHAPTER **11**

ADX GAPPER

This is a simple retracement pattern which lets us enter in the direction of a trending market. It is similar to other types of gap-reversal strategies except that it uses the ADX and +DI/–DI as a filter, thus increasing the overall profitability of trading gaps.

Again, the ADX measures the strength of the trend over time. +DI and –DI indicate the direction of the trend. If the trend is up, the +DI will be higher than the –DI and vice versa. We want to use the ADX to identify periods where the trend is strong, to wait for days that gap in the opposite direction of the trend, and then to climb aboard if the market resumes its original trend.

Here are the rules for this strategy:

1. We will use a 12-period ADX and a 28-period +DI/–DI. (Night sessions are omitted.)

2. The ADX must be greater than 30.

3. For buys, the +DI must be greater than the –DI; for sells, the –DI must be greater than the +DI.

FOR BUYS (SELLS ARE REVERSED)

1. Today's open must gap below yesterday's low.

2. A buy stop is placed in the area of yesterday's low.

3. If filled, a protective sell stop is placed at today's low.

4. Lock in profits with a trailing stop and either exit the position before the close or carry it into the following day if it closes strongly.

Here are three trades that occured during a three-week span in July 95 Cotton.

EXHIBIT 11.1 Cotton—July 1995

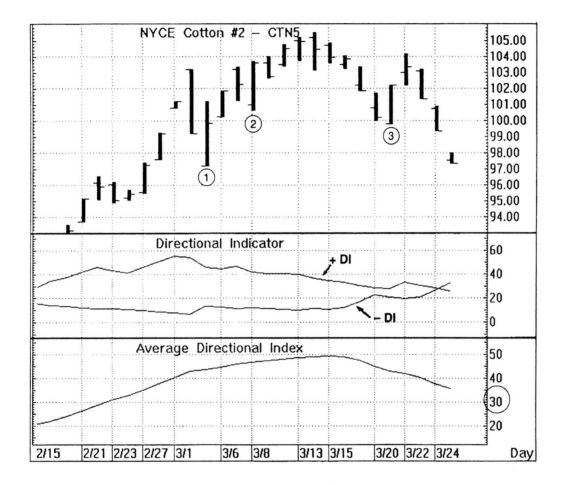

1. March 3, 1995, cotton has a 12-period ADX above 30 and the +DI is above the −DI signifying an uptrend. The market gaps lower. A buy stop is placed in the area of the previous day's low of 99.15. The market rallies to as high as 101.18 and closes at 99.85.

2. On March 6, cotton again gaps lower and reverses. A buy stop at yesterday's low of 101.65 is triggered. Cotton proceeds to close 190 points higher.

3. Another lower gap and profitable reversal.

EXHIBIT 11.2 Wheat—December 1995

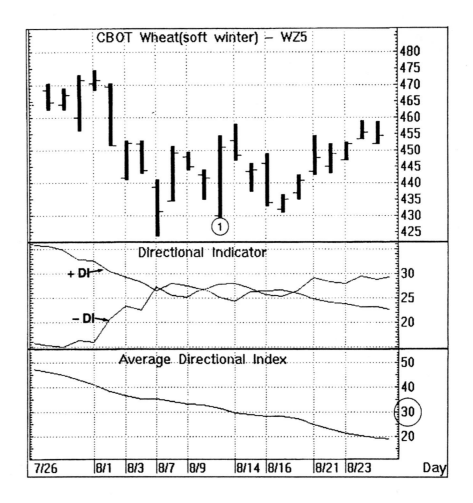

During the summer of 1995, wheat experiences a contra-seasonal bull market. On August 11, December wheat gaps lower and reverses. A buy stop is triggered at the previous day's low of 435. A protective trailing sell stop is placed just under today's low of 429. The market closes 16 cents above our buy stop.

EXHIBIT 11.3 S&P—June 1995

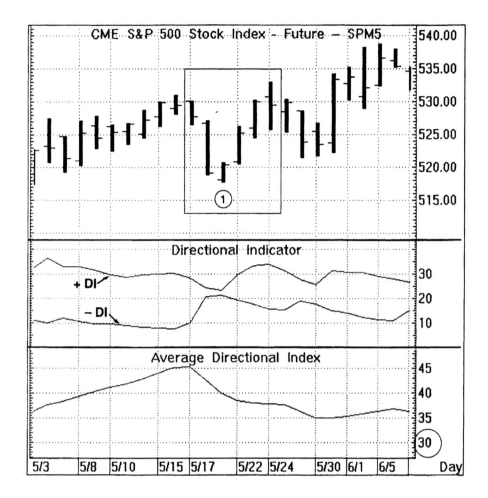

The bull market of 1995 led to a setup on May 19. With the ADX above 30 and +DI above −DI, the market gaps lower and reverses. A buy stop is triggered at 518.90. The market closes near the high of the day. Traders have the option of taking profits or carrying the position overnight. (As you can see, the upward bias continues with the S&P trading five points higher the next day.) Back testing of this strategy shows profit improvement holding these trades into the next morning.

Let's walk through a trade that I (Larry) took while finishing the manual.

EXHIBIT 11.4 Orange Juice—January 1996

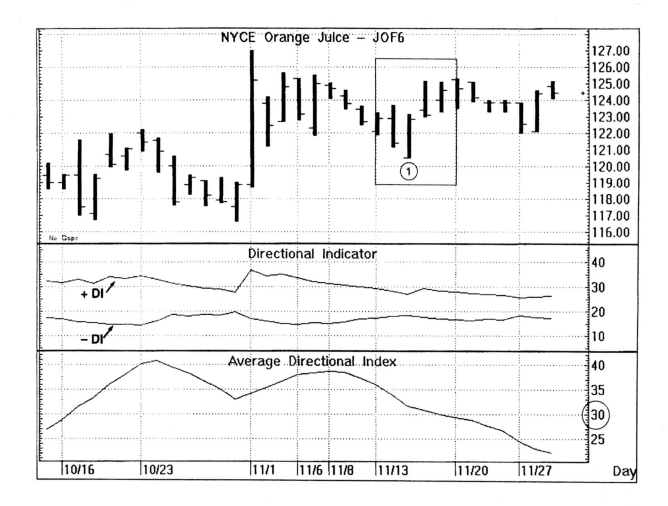

1. November 15, 1995 (gap day), January orange juice has a 12-period ADX above 30 and the +DI is above the –DI, signifying an uptrend.

2. The market gaps lower. A buy stop is placed at 121.20, one tick above the previous day's low. Once filled, an initial protective sell stop is placed one tick below this morning's low of 120.50.

3. The market rallies up to 123.00. The stop is trailed up to 122.10 to lock in profits.

4. As we enter the final hour of trading, there is a profit. In this scenario, I moved the stop to 122.60. The market holds so I remain long overnight. I know from experience that this strong close will have a high likelihood of following through the next morning.

5. In the first 15 minutes, the market opens higher and trades as high as 124.55. I immediately place a stop at 124.00 and get filled at 123.80.

EXHIBIT 11.5 Orange Juice—January 1996 Intraday

LINDA:

Gaps usually represent some sort of extreme in emotion. They are also very visible chart patterns to other market participants. Why not just trade all gaps?

LARRY:

Larry Williams proved that trading gap reversals is a statistically correct strategy (see Appendix). He called these reversals "Oops trades." I traded the Oops strategy for awhile and made money with it, but I found that most of my profits were coming from a small handful of trades.

LINDA:

And you looked for a common denominator among those winning trades?

LARRY:

Yes. My best gains were coming from strongly trending markets. By selling higher gaps in bear markets, I am basically climbing aboard for the downward ride, and a number of times it is really quite a ride. (The same holds true for buying lower gaps and riding the market as it rises.)

LINDA:

You mean because of the follow-through?

LARRY:

Yes. There are a handful of times each year which bring substantial one- to five-day profits.

LINDA:

How many times a year do the ADX gap reversals setup?

LARRY:

The ADX filter reduces the number of gap reversal trades. If you follow all the active markets like I do, you will get between two to four trades per week.

LINDA:

You also trade these reversals without gaps. How does that work?

LARRY:

That is more subjective. Let's assume the ADX is above 30 and the trend is up. I will look for some early morning weakness in the market, perhaps a down opening. If the market begins to recover and moves above yesterday's close, I will buy. I firmly believe this is a conceptually correct strategy to trade. The market is attempting to sell off in the morning, but because the overall trend is so strong, the uptrend resumes and I want to be part of that continuation.

LINDA:

Where is your initial protective stop?

LARRY:

Usually at today's morning low. I will then move it higher as my position becomes profitable, or if the market becomes very dull. Ideally, I want to see the market explode higher; otherwise, I will just scratch the trade.

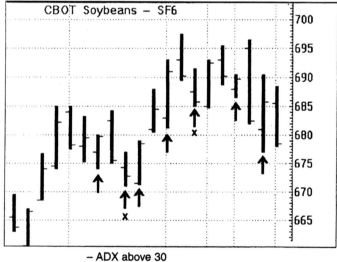

- ADX above 30
- Trend up
- Opening weakness and reversal
  x = Losing trade

PART THREE

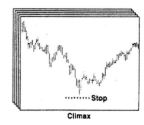

CLIMAX PATTERNS

CHAPTER 12

WHIPLASH

This is a simple strategy that takes advantage of gaps by entering on the close (MOC) if specific criteria are met. It is also unique in that the gap does not need to be filled. We are looking for days when a gap in the morning is followed by a reversal in the afternoon. This reversal tends to follow-through the next morning and often for the next few days. We must wait until the close to enter as we want confirmation that the market has truly failed.

BUY SETUP (SELLS ARE REVERSED)

1. The market must gap lower than the previous day's low. (Night sessions are omitted.)

2. The close must be higher than the opening and also in the top 50 percent of the day's trading range.

3. If rules 1 and 2 are met, buy MOC.

4. If tomorrow opens below today's close (indicating a loss on the position), sell immediately! Take the loss!

5. If tomorrow opens with a profit, trail a stop to protect profits.

It might seem odd to enter on the close, only to get out on a bad opening. However, more often than not the market will open favorably the next day, and it is these small profits we are playing to capture. Back testing indicates a good win/loss percentage in the overnight gap action. It is very easy to manage the winning trades, so we consider this to be a good enough "headstart!" At the very least, you would not want to be on the opposite side of this trade.

Now let's look at some examples.

EXHIBIT 12.1 Soybeans—November 1995

Here are four examples from a three-week period in soybeans:

1. Soybeans gap higher, the close is below the opening and in the bottom 50 percent of its daily range—sell MOC at 659 1/4. The next morning the market opens lower at 656. Tight stops are placed to protect profits. (Where you place your stops is a personal choice. Just do not let this profit turn into a loss!)

2. Soybeans gap lower, close in the top half of its range and close above the opening. We will buy MOC at 656 1/4. The next morning the market opens 1 1/4 cents higher (its low for the day) and rallies nearly 10 cents from the previous day's close.

3. Soybeans gap higher, close below their opening and close in the bottom half of their range. Sell MOC. The next morning, Soybeans open at a small profit. Stops should be trailed appropriately.

4. A whiplash setup to the sell side.

LINDA:

Do you trade this strategy in all markets?

LARRY:

I am aware of it in all markets, but I tend to trade it more often in the S&Ps and bonds.

LINDA:

It seems that people are often intimidated by gaps. Some traders do not feel comfortable with the usual accompanying increase in volatility.

LARRY:

That's why it's so important to continually look for systematic rules to exploit these gaps. It's a constant process of discovering the most probable course of action for the market.

LINDA:

O.K. What tendency are you exploiting here?

LARRY:

This strategy is tied to the fact that days which reverse from market extremes tend to have follow-through the next morning.

LINDA:

That's right. When a setup gives you an almost 60 percent headstart, as this one does, the chance to make money is very good. There also seems to be a slight sell-side bias to this strategy.

LARRY:

Yes, the testing confirms this also.

CHAPTER **13**

THREE-DAY UNFILLED GAP REVERSALS

Here is another pattern which employs a gap-reversal strategy. In this particular case, the market must begin to close an unfilled gap within three days.

BUY SETUP (SELLS ARE REVERSED)

1. Today the market must gap lower and not fill the gap. (As with every other strategy in this book, night sessions are omitted.)

2. Over the next three trading sessions, have in place a buy stop one tick above the high of the gap-down day.

3. If filled, place a protective sell stop at the low of the gap-down day.

4. Protect any accrued profits with a trailing stop. Often a market will close a gap and then reverse again.

5. If not filled after three trading sessions, cancel the initial buy stop.

EXHIBIT 13.1 Wheat—March 1995

1. An unfilled gap higher. A resting sell stop is placed for the next three trading sessions at 394 1/4, one tick below today's low.

2. Our sell stop is filled and our protective buy stop is placed at 400 1/4, one tick above the unfilled gap-day high.

3. We are stopped out for a six cents loss plus slippage and commission.

4. An unfilled gap. We place a sell stop one tick below today's low of 405 3/4 for the next three trading days.

5. We are filled and our protective buy stop is placed at 410, one tick above the gap day's high.

6. The market sells off over 20 cents during the next seven sessions.

Here are three trades that occurred over a one-month period in Motorola.

1. An unfilled gap. We buy the next day, one tick above today's high. As you can see, the market rallies strongly over the next few days.

2. Another unfilled gap that begins to get filled the next day. We sell Motorola short in the 76 area and the market drops over eight points in two days.

3. The gap from 7–19 is filled in two days. The market trades five points higher over the next three days.

Also, let's look at the money-management rules for this example. Because the low of 7–19 is 6 1/2 points below our entry, our protective sell stop must be placed at a higher level. Our recommendation is to risk in the range of two to three points with this trade.

EXHIBIT 13.2 Motorola (MOT)—1995

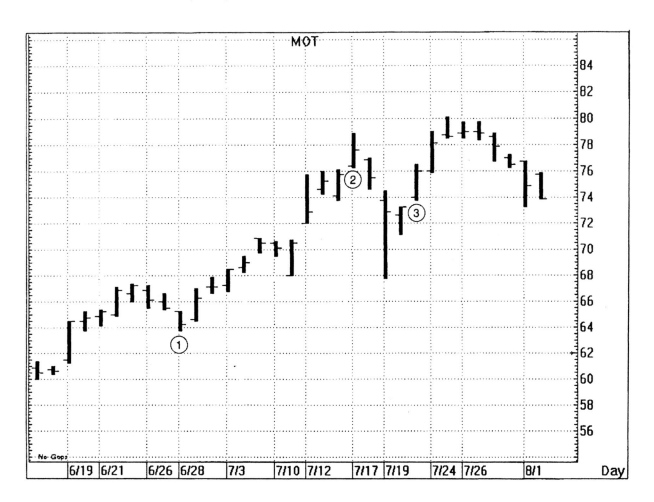

106   Chapter 13

EXHIBIT 13.3 Orange Juice—March 1995

1. December 19, 1994, an unfilled gap.

2. Orange juice trades below the December 19 low. We are short with a protective stop at 123.80.

3. Orange juice loses 10 cents in six-trading sessions.

EXHIBIT 13.4 Soybean Meal—March 1995

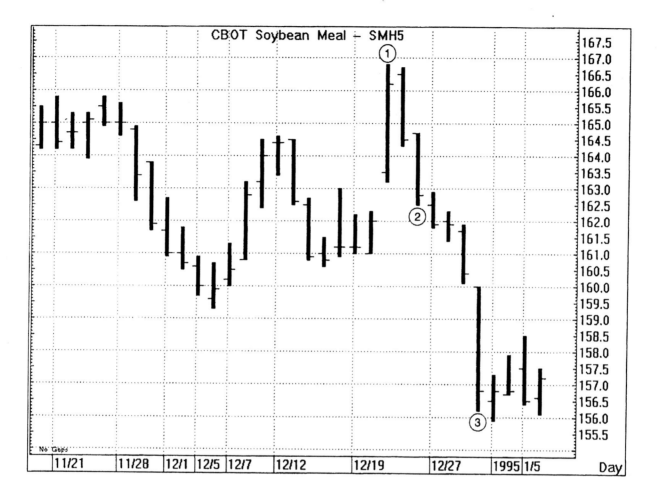

1. An unfilled gap higher.

2. We short one tick below the gap day's low. (In case you missed the Turtle Soup Plus One sell signal the previous day!)

3. Soybean meal loses over 600 points in five-trading sessions.

LINDA:

Is this another example of markets reaching short-term extremes and reversing?

LARRY:

Yes, these types of gap extremes occur when markets are either overreacting to news or are in exhaustive phases.

LINDA:

Like island reversals?

LARRY:

That's right. Once a gap begins to get filled, the momentum often picks up, and the moves are potentially significant.

LINDA:

It seems to me that with this setup you go through periods of small gains and small losses, and then you participate when the reversal is significant.

LARRY:

Exactly.

LINDA:

Why three days? Why not six days or 20 days?

LARRY:

Remember, we are trading on a short-term time frame. Also, in my opinion, a gap that occurred 20 days ago is less significant than one that occurred yesterday.

LINDA:

This obviously works nicely in equities.

LARRY:

Yes, it does. In fact, the strategy seems to work best in momentum stocks. The more volatile the stock, the more significant this pattern is.

CHAPTER **14**

A PICTURE'S WORTH A THOUSAND WORDS

The following are three distinctive reversal patterns. They are **climax** patterns, which means the reversal occurs from buying or selling exhaustion. Each of the patterns has a **setup** so that you can **anticipate** the market's reversal. This setup also prevents you from entering a trending market prematurely. The real beauty of these patterns is that they all form a distinctive risk point where you can place a stop. Once the market reverses from these points, it should not look back until some profits can be locked in.

These patterns are a purely **subjective** form of pattern recognition. This means that it is impossible to do any form of back testing on them. It is also difficult to describe precise rules or placement of resting orders for entry as we have done on previous setups. The best advice is to study these examples and then look for similar patterns on your own charts. All three of these patterns set up in any market on any timeframe.

Since many of our friends have been able to trade from these patterns, we know they are easily recognizable. In fact, "Three Little Indians" was originally taught by two fellow traders who trade from tick charts. A word of advice: the people who trade subjective chart patterns spend many hours after the market closes reexamining examples that were set up during that day's session. They also concentrate very hard on trading only two or three specific setups. They do not use oscillators or moving averages as they insist on being purists. (This chapter could have been titled, "TRADING—THE SCHOOL OF MINIMALISM!")

The best technique to use when entering these trades calls for some good old-fashioned tape reading or monitoring the charts right when the anticipated reversal is occurring. You must concentrate first on seeing the **risk** point or logical spot to put your stop before you enter the trade. Once you see the swing low that the market should not come down to again (in the case of a buy), pick up the phone and buy at-the-market. Do not try to price the trade because the odds are too high that you will miss it. The best entries from these three setups have a small window of opportunity.

An easy way to exit these trades is to wait until the market begins to give back any gains or stalls in its movement; then exit at-the-market. They are also easy setups in which to trail a stop in order to lock in profits. Don't forget, trailing a stop is an active trading process. You must monitor new support or resistance levels as they are being formed and then move your resting stop up to just below/above these levels. Orders can be given as "Cancel–Replace," which means you don't forget to cancel your previous resting stop order. Never let yourself be exposed to runaway market conditions without **resting** orders in the market, as any one of the patterns can reverse at any time!

EXHIBIT 14.1 Gold—30-Minute

This first pattern is called "spike and ledge." Here, a buying climax forms a spike and ledge pattern on an intraday gold chart. A short trade is entered on the breakdown out of the ledge at point 1 and an initial stop is placed on the other side of the ledge. The market should not come back to this level. The market closes its gap and we probably would have exited the trade on the small range expansion bar at point 2.

EXHIBIT 14.2 S&P—15-Minute

A dramatic selling climax forms a spike at point A. We buy the breakout from the following ledge at point 1 and place our stop on the other side of the ledge at level B. A range expansion bar at point 2 signals the move has temporarily exhausted itself.

EXHIBIT 14.3 S&P—10-Tick

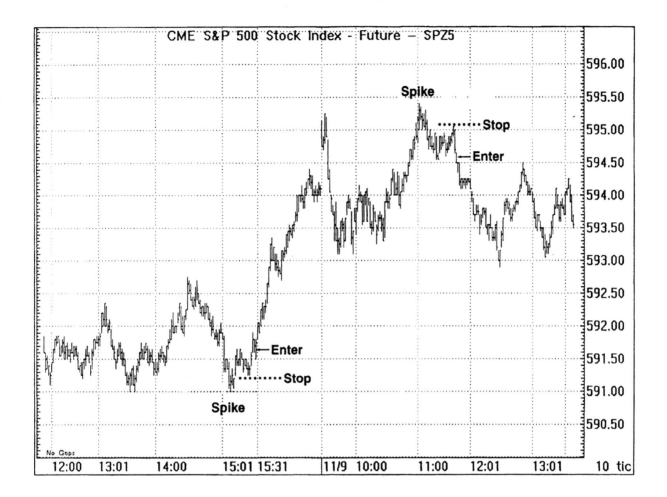

Spike and ledge patterns work great on all time frames. Notice how both of these trades were tests of a previous low and high.

EXHIBIT 14.4 Bonds—December 1995

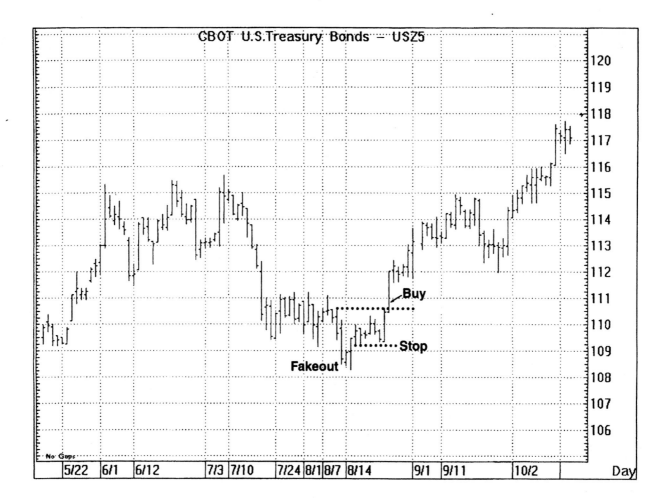

This pattern is called the "Fakeout—Shakeout." Once a market breaks from a ledge or a triangle, it should not come back to the breakout point, or the apex of the triangle. If it does, it sets up an excellent trade in the *other direction*. The market has fooled and trapped the majority of the participants. In this particular example, a buy stop is placed just above the point from which the market broke down. The initial stop is entered at the most recent swing low. The market should not come back to this point. The stop is quickly moved up to breakeven, and then trailed appropriately to lock in profits.

EXHIBIT 14.5 S&P—20-Tick

The market broke from a narrow-range ledge that had been forming for three hours (11:00 to 2:00). The shorts were faked out and the longs were shaken out! A legitimate breakout should not come back to the midpoint of the ledge. If it does, it signals that the breakout was a trap. We want to be on board when it reverses direction. In this case, we picked up the phone and bought at-the-market when it came out the other side. Our stop was very quickly moved up to breakeven.

116 Chapter 14

EXHIBIT 14.6 S&P—60-Minute

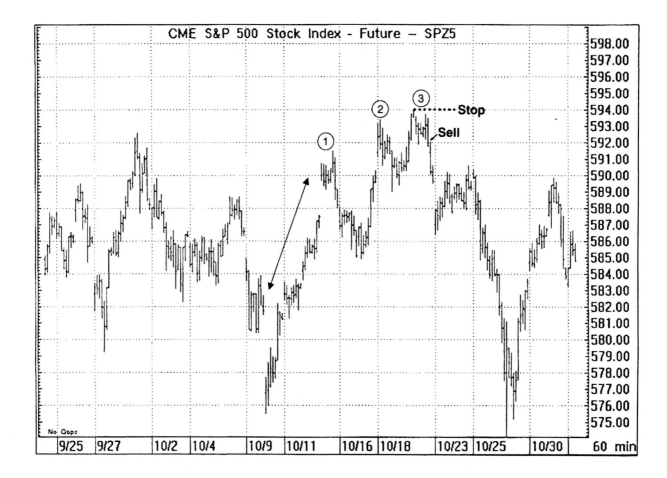

Three Little Indians is a climax pattern formed by three symmetrical peaks. We can anticipate the third peak being formed, but must wait for the price to **reverse** off the last peak before we enter. We can then place our stop in the market at the **same time** we enter our position. We enter at-the-market—if we try to price our entry on any of these patterns shown intraday, too often we will miss the trade. The stop should quickly be moved to breakeven. The winning trades do not look back. They should reward us instantly.

EXHIBIT 14.7 Coffee—30-Minute

Three Little Indians—coffee formed three symmetrical peaks after a six-day rally. The price starts to reverse and we enter the trade at-the-market. Our initial stop, at the most recent swing high, can be quickly moved to breakeven. The market closed weak so we carry the trade overnight. The next morning we cover our short position on the range expansion bar at point 4. We were in the market less than four hours total.

EXHIBIT 14.8 S&P—5-Tick

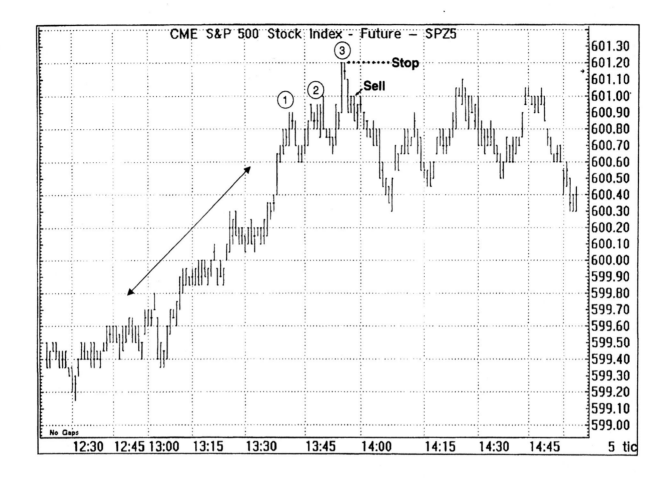

This is a classic example of a Three Little Indians climax at the end of a strong move. A small profit was made on the trade, which is all that we should expect when trading on a five-tick chart!

EXHIBIT 14.9 Heating Oil—January 1996

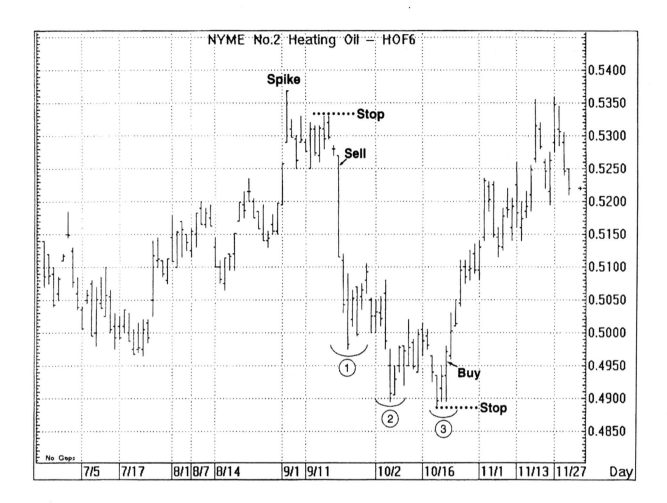

Here is a good example of both the Spike and Ledge setup and the Three Little Indians on a daily bar chart. Both trades gave us a good initial place to put our stop, and both moved quickly in our favor.

CHAPTER **15**

WOLFE WAVES

This particular methodology is perhaps the most unique, effective trading technique I've (Linda) ever come across! It was developed and shared by a good friend, Bill Wolfe, who for the last 10 years has made a living trading the S&P. His son, Brian, also trades it. Brian was the first teenager I've ever met who consistently made a good income scalping NYFE (Knife) futures from his apartment. Brian, now 21, has expanded into trading the Wolfe Wave in other markets.

Bill's theory of wave structure is based on Newton's first law of physics: for every action there is an opposite reaction. This movement creates a definite wave with valuable projecting capabilities. This wave most clearly sets up when there is good volatility. With a bit of practice, it is easy to train your eye to spot these patterns instantly.

The following rules will make sense when you examine the examples. (Please note the odd sequence in counting. As you will see, it is necessary for the inductive analysis.)

By starting with a top or bottom on the bar chart, we are assured of beginning our count on a new wave. This count is for a **buy** setup. We begin the count at a top. (The wave count would be reversed if we were starting at the bottom looking for a **sell** setup).

1. Number 2 wave is a top.

2. Number 3 wave is the bottom of a first decline.

3. Number 1 wave is the bottom prior to wave 2 (top). Point 3 must be lower than point 1.

4. Number 4 wave is the top of wave 3. The wave 4 point should be higher than the wave 1 bottom.

5. A trend line is drawn from point 1 to point 3. The extension of this line projects to the anticipated reversal point which we will call wave 5. **this is the entry point for a ride to the epa line** (1 to 4).

6. The Estimated Price at Arrival (EPA) is the trend line drawn from points 1 to 4. This projects the anticipated price objective. Our initial stop is placed just beneath the newly formed reversal at point 5. It can then be quickly moved to breakeven.

IMPORTANT POINT: You cannot begin looking for the Wolfe Wave until points 1, 2, 3, and 4 have been formed. Keep in mind that point 3 **must** be lower than point 1 for a buy setup. It must be higher than point 1 for a sell setup. Also, on the best waves point 4 will be higher than point 1 for a buy setup and lower than 1 for a sell setup. This ensures that absolute runaway market conditions do not exist.

Now, study the examples and see if you can train your eye to begin to see the Wolfe Wave setup.

Exhibit 15.1 illustrates what a Wolfe Wave looks like when it is starting to form.

Point 1, 2, and 3 must already have formed. Point 2 must be a significant swing low or high. A trend line is then drawn between points 1 and 3. This projects where we should anticipate point 5.

EXHIBIT 15.1 S&P—60-Minute Detail

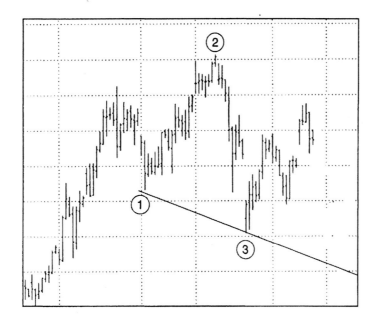

Point 5 is formed. We will buy the reversal from this area and place a tight stop underneath. If we draw a trend line from point 1 to point 4, it should give us a price projection.

EXHIBIT 15.1A S&P 60-Minute Detail

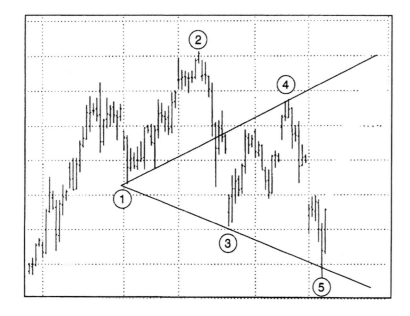

124 Chapter 15

EXHIBIT 15.2 S&P—60-Minute

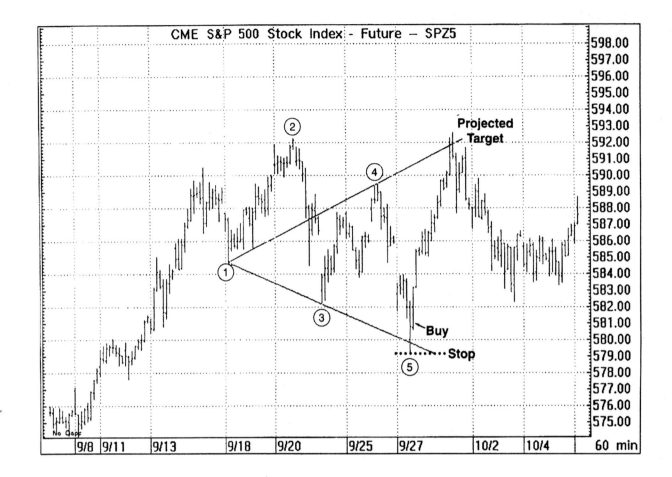

The price meets its objective for a potential gain of 12 points!

EXHIBIT 15.3 Sugar—10-Tick

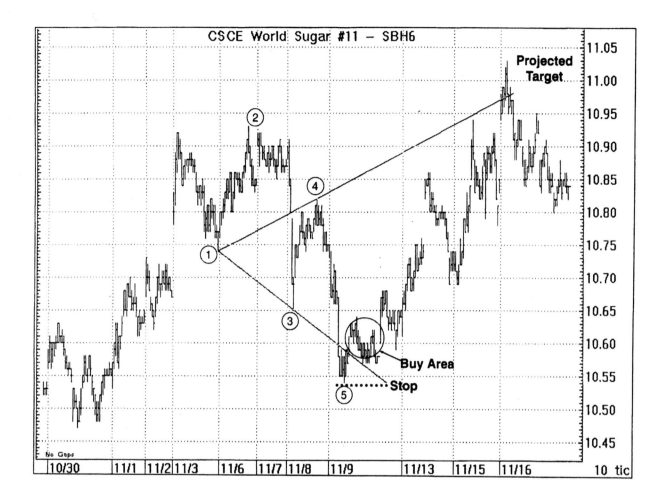

Point 2 is the initial starting point for the pattern. I always find it easiest to start the count at this point. Then, backtrack and find point 1 and 3. Don't forget that point 4 must be higher than point 1. Our trend line is drawn projecting point 5. The market finds support at this level, so we enter a long position at-the-market and place a stop just below point 5. The market trades to its objective.

EXHIBIT 15.4 S&P—5-Minute

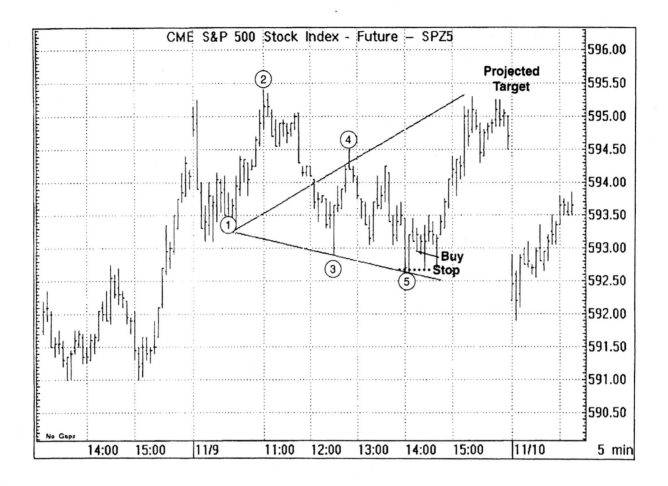

Here is an example of the Wolfe Wave on a five-minute chart. We find three to six setups a week in the S&Ps in this time frame.

A trend line connecting points 1 and 3 projects our buying area. It is very common for the market to overshoot point 5 by a small margin, so you **must** wait for the price to reverse back above the trendline **before** initiating a trade. In this example, we buy at-the-market and place a stop beneath the low. The market then rallys two points over the next hour!

EXHIBIT 15.5 Canadian Dollar—December 1995

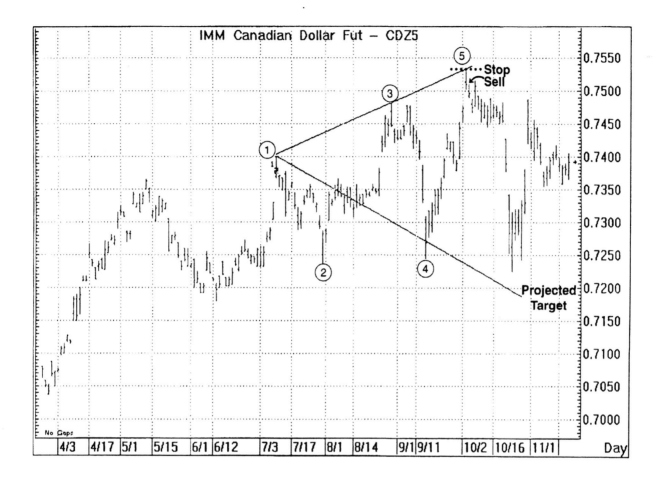

Point 2 is our starting point for the count. (We can only find point 2 after points 1 and 3 have already formed.) Point 2 does not have to be a long-term trend reversal, only a significant swing high or low.

My friend Dan sent me this chart when point 5 had formed. I shook my head and said the market felt so strong—how could it possibly break down! It came darned close to meeting the projection. I don't think anyone could have imagined this scenario at the time. (Notice the spike and ledge pattern the market broke from!)

EXHIBIT 15.6 Boeing (BA)—1995

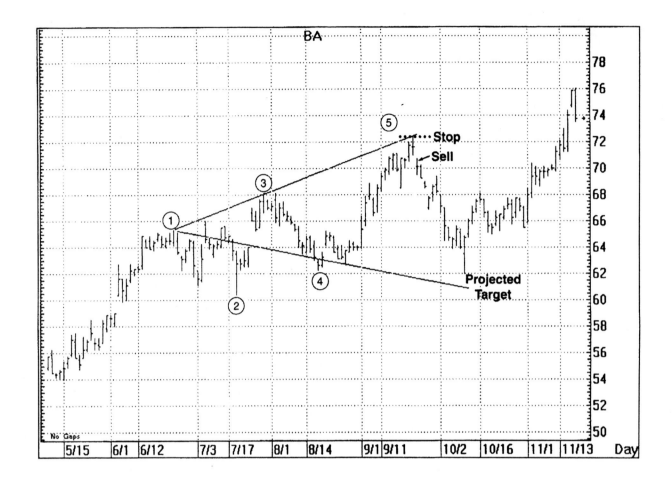

Here is an example on a stock chart. Point 2 is a significant swing low. Point 4 is lower than point 1. A trend line connecting 1 and 3 projects point 5 where the market meets the price objective to the tick! Again, as in the Canadian dollar, the trade did not quite meet its projected downside target. However, there was plenty of opportunity to take some profits out of this 10-point drop.

EXHIBIT 15.7 SPZ—10-Tick

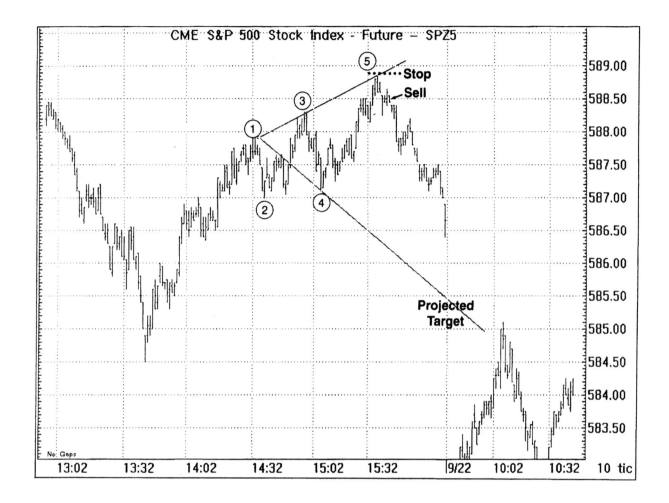

Wolfe Waves sometimes set up on Three Little Indians. Look back in Chapter 14 and see if you can see the waves on Examples 14.7 and 14.8.

LINDA:

It took me awhile to get the hang of spotting this pattern. Now I try to look for them on all my charts. I have a lot of fun watching them develop.

Everyone in my office was watching the 60-minute S&P example shown earlier take shape. None of us could believe it when the projected objective was met. A local group of Wolfe Wave practitioners began to **fax** the chart to each other. Of course, none of us actually caught the whole move. Some of us were lucky and used the pattern to exit a short trade at point 5, but Brian actually went long right at the bottom!

CHAPTER 16

NEWS

ESPN basketball analyst Dick Vitale would make a great trader. We can see him sitting in front of the screen screaming, "Talk to me, baby!" And you know what? The screen would probably talk back and Vitale would make a fortune.

The markets talk to us all the time. For example, let's look at December 1994. The Federal Reserve raised interest rates, California's Orange County was teetering on the verge of bankruptcy, and Mexico was in the midst of an economic freefall after the devaluation of the peso. Any rational investor would assume that our equity market should go down. Let's look at this using the same logic the press uses. Higher interest rates? Stocks go down. Municipal bonds default? Stocks go down. Our trading neighbor devalues its currency? Stocks go down. All three the same month? Stocks really go down!

In reality though, the market did not go down. The S&P 500 finished 1.5 percent higher for the month. **What was the market saying?** It was saying, "I don't care about higher interest rates or an economic crisis, **I'm going higher!**" And that is in fact what happened. Over the next 10 months, the Dow Jones appreciated over 30 percent.

132   Chapter 16

This type of market talk occurs all the time. Let's look at an example of a day-trading opportunity that occurred on September 13, 1995. The S&P future was up a few points when IBM, one of the stocks that led the 1995 bull market, told analysts it would not meet earnings expectations. Logically, this should have hurt the market. Here is the leading technology stock in a high-tech industry driven market telling analysts business is not as good as everyone thought. IBM sold off sharply after the news release, and the S&P's initially lost 2 1/2 points. However, the sell-off was quickly shrugged off as the market said, **"I don't care about IBM, I'm going higher!"** The S&Ps immediately reversed and rallied three points. The next day it rose another five points!

EXHIBIT 16.1 IBM—September 13, 1995

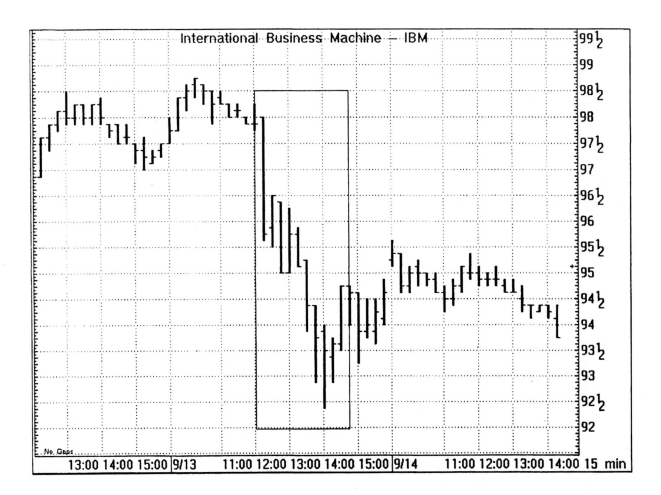

EXHIBIT 16.2 S&P—September 13, 1995

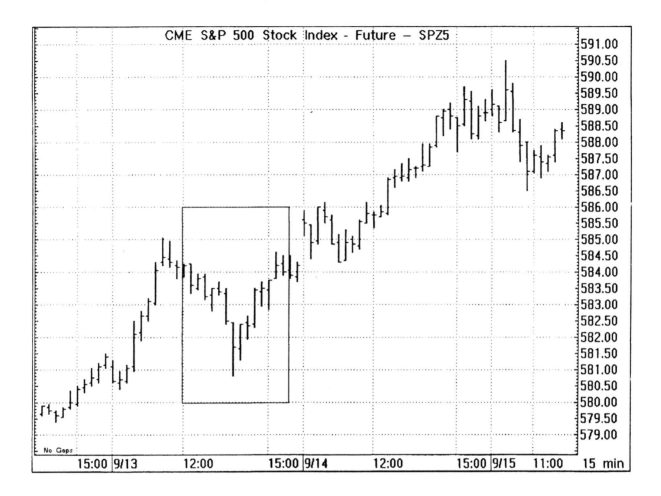

The ability to trade by using reverse logic is not easy. You must discard all your preconceived notions and opinions in order to truly listen to the market and recognize when it is acting like a contrarian. If you can do this, it is one of the most valuable trading concepts. A well-known market wizard said that nearly half of the 100 million dollars he made from trading came from the times he was able to identify when the market was defying the so-called logic and moved in the opposite direction.

This concept can also be applied to seasonals. Some of the best trends can be counter-seasonal moves. Just look at how the wheat market in the summer of 1995 defied the normal downside bias. The bottom line is, instead of trying to show the market how smart you are, take a step back and let it talk to you! It's much smarter to observe the market's response to a news event, seasonal tendency, or technical setup than it is to attempt to impose your beliefs on it. This is what true street smarts is really all about.

Logical thinking will lead you right to the poor house. The majority of traders in the United States (us included) were raised in some version of a typical American upbringing. We went to school for 12 years, went to our proms, played organized sports, belonged to a youth social group, etc. Many of us then went on to a four-year college preparing for employment or graduate school. No matter how much you want to believe you are an individual, the overwhelming evidence shows that your thought process is not that much different from most other traders. This type of upbringing allows you to see the world logically, and it is this logic which is used by thousands and thousands of traders to make decisions: bad crop report—soybean prices logically go up, bad inflation news—bond prices logically go down. There is no trading edge whatsoever in trying to base decisions on what the market should logically be doing. In fact, the more logical something is, the more likely you will lose when the market is moving in the opposite direction of the prevailing logic.

Now let's look at two specific strategies you can profit by when trading against the prevailing logic.

CHAPTER **17**

MORNING NEWS REVERSALS

Economic news reports in the morning are notorious for causing erratic price behavior upon their release. It is often a time of great uncertainty, and the ensuing volatility creates opportunity. This strategy will take advantage of the violent price behavior. Here are the rules:

1. Wait for an economic news event to be released at 8:30 EST. The report can be the unemployment numbers, the consumer price index, producer price index, GDP report, etc. The more significant the report, the better the trading opportunity.

2. Identify the previous day's high and low for the bond market.

3. If the report immediately lifts the bond market at least four ticks above the previous day's high, place a sell-stop one to three ticks underneath the previous day's high. (If the bond market trades below the previous day's low by four ticks, place a buy-stop one to three ticks above the previous day's low.)

4. If filled, place an initial protective stop one tick above today's high (or for buys, one tick below today's low). As the position becomes profitable, immediately move the stop to breakeven.

136   Chapter 17

5. The same strategy can be used in the currencies. If they trade 10–20 ticks beyond the previous day's extreme, place a stop 5–10 ticks on the other side of the previous day's extreme. Move your stop to breakeven as soon as it becomes profitable.

Let's look at a few trades from a two-week period in November 1995.

EXHIBIT 17.1 Bonds—December 1995

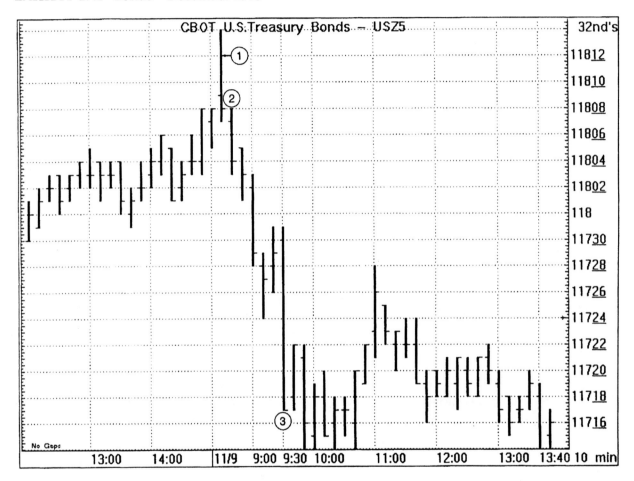

1. The government reports that the producer price index was down 0.1 percent for the month of October signaling low inflation. Bonds immediately trade at least four ticks above the previous day's high of 118-08.

2. We place a sell-stop in the 118-06 range and are immediately filled. A protective buy-stop is placed one tick above today's high of 118-14.

3. The sell-off is significant. Within one hour we get a parabolic drop. Bonds trade to as low as 117-17. We will tighten our stops to assure locking in the profit.

EXHIBIT 17.2 Bonds—December 1995

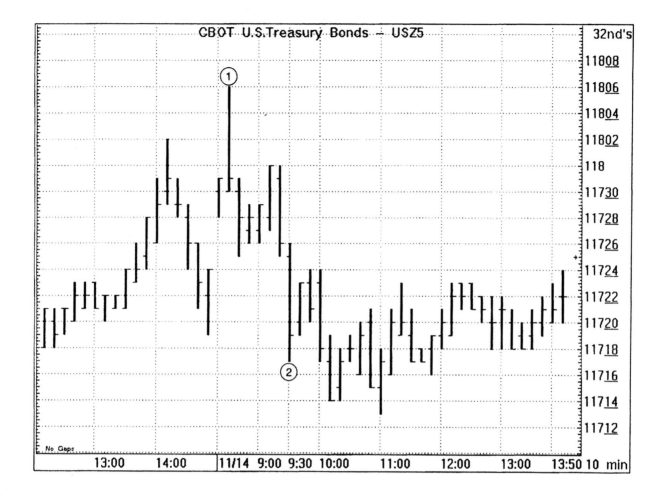

1. Retail sales for October are reported showing the economy is slowing down. Bonds immediately rise at least four ticks above the previous day's high and reverse. A sell-stop is placed in the 118-00 range and we are short. A protective buy-stop is placed at 118-07, one tick above today's high.

2. The market trades to as low as 117-17. Our stop is trailed to protect profits.

EXHIBIT 17.3 Swiss Franc—December 1995

1. November 3, 1995, the U.S. employment report shows an unexpected increase in nonfarm jobs. The Swiss franc immediately sells off and then reverses. A buy-stop is placed in the 87.75 range, a few ticks above the previous day's low. Upon being filled, a protective sell-stop is placed at 87.57.

2. The reversal is sharp and our trailing stop is raised. The Swiss franc trades more than 40 points higher within 20 minutes.

LINDA:

How did you arrive at this strategy?

LARRY:

I noticed how many times the bond market had initial sharp reactions to significant economic events in the morning and then reversed.

LINDA:

This has been going on for years. The bond market is notorious for reversals on these days.

LARRY:

That's right. And by having a structured plan to participate in these reversals, it keeps you from guessing whether or not the market will actually reverse.

LINDA:

Do you find it psychologically tough to trade this strategy?

LARRY:

Yes. The initial reaction off the news is usually the logical reaction. For example, if the inflation numbers are poor, it is logical to expect bonds to sell-off. The media's interpretation of the report will reinforce this logic even further.

LINDA:

On the trading floor, we always tested the axiom, "Buy the rumor, sell the news!"

LARRY:

You can't use logic to trade this strategy. Otherwise, if you do, you will never be successful with it. It is very tough to put in a buy-stop in bonds when the so-called experts are telling you the bonds are going down.

LINDA:

What happens if you get stopped out with a loss and the bonds reverse again? Will you attempt to reenter your position at the original point?

LARRY:

Good question. Yes, I have found some of my best gains come from reentering the position. There are times the market can't decide which way it wants to go, but once it does decide, the move is significant!

CHAPTER **18**

BIG PICTURE NEWS REVERSALS

Big picture news reversals are a longer-term strategy (as opposed to scalping off morning economic news reports).

They require patience to monitor the initial setup but often lead to a trade that you can hold for many weeks. They tend to set up most frequently in the equity markets, but are just as easily tradable in commodities.

1. We are looking for an extraordinary event to occur which causes a market to move dramatically. (The examples are what we consider to be extraordinary events.)

2. Identify the market's last closing price before the event occurred that caused it to have the sharp move.

3. Place a resting stop order to enter the market at this previous closing price level. If the market can digest the radical event and come back to this closing price level, we want to participate in the reversing move.

4. Risk with a stop up to the lowest level the stock reached after the sell off. For example, if a stock was trading at 20 before the event and it then sold off to 17, we will buy the stock if it comes back to 20 and risk down to 17.

EXHIBIT 18.1 Intel (INTC)—1994

1. On December 8, 1994, Intel acknowledged that their Pentium chip did not calculate extended number computations correctly (an extraordinary event to say the least). The stock, which was trading at 65 before the news, sells off more than 10 percent over the next eight days. After the sell-off, the stock begins to rebound. We look to buy if it trades in the 65 area.

2. On January 5, Intel reaches our buy point. After purchasing the stock, we place a protective sell-stop at 57 1/2, INTC's post-news low.

EXHIBIT 18.2 Intel (INTC)—1995

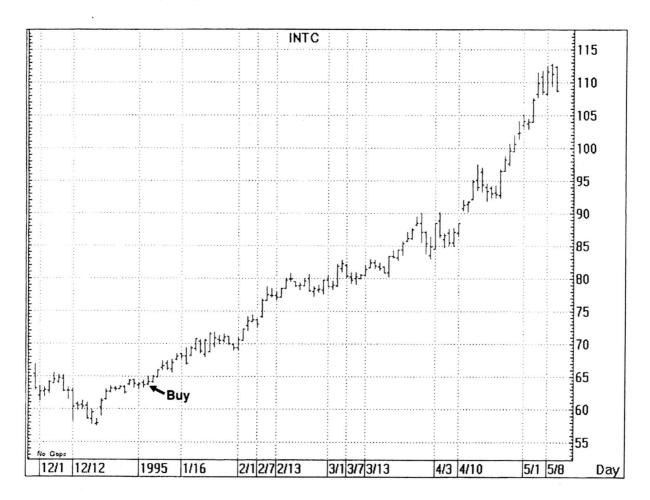

As you can see, over the next 6 1/2 months Intel's stock price appreciates over 80 percent.

Here is another example from late 1994.

On December 5, 1994, Orange County, California, one of the wealthiest communities in the United States, announces that their investment fund has lost over $100 million. A default on their bonds is possible. MBIA, an insurer of municipal bonds and a large insurer of Orange County bonds, now has a problem. Over the next few days, panic sets in. MBIA sells off nearly 10 percent This extraordinary event is the setup for our big picture news reversal. On December 8, MBIA recovers to the pre-news sell-off price (point 1 on the chart). A buy order is executed. A protective sell-stop is placed at its post-news event low of 47 1/4. As you can see, MBIA rises nearly 20 percent over the next two months and nearly 40 percent over the next half of a year.

Let's stop for a second and look at this example from a psychological viewpoint. This is not an easy trade to take, especially if you live is Southern California! The press is all over this story. The local papers and *The Wall Street Journal* had this crisis as their lead story on a daily basis.

EXHIBIT 18.3 MBIA (MBI)

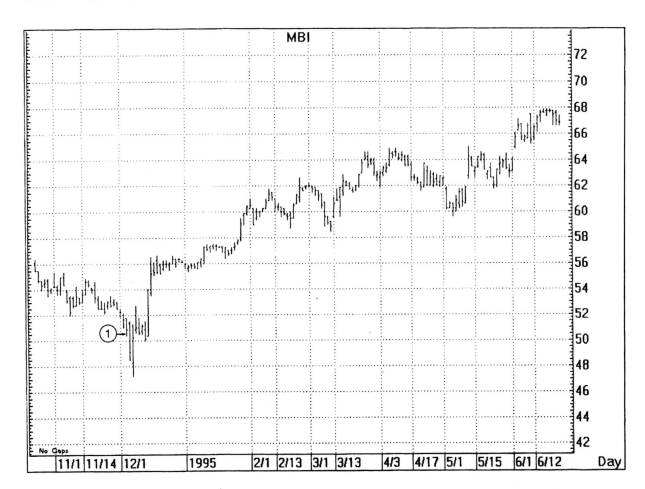

You could not turn on a news program without hearing all the experts making dire predictions for this situation. On top of all this, you could not even get bids for most Orange County bonds from the brokerage houses! The logical and safe thing to do was to stand aside. But, in hindsight, the trade was terrific! The stock was telling you, "I don't care about a default possibility, I'm going higher!"

By listening to what the stock was saying instead of what the experts (who were thinking logically) were telling you, you would have made a solid return on the trade.

EXHIBIT 18.4 Motorola (MOT)—1993

In January 1993, rumors abounded that cellular telephones caused cancer. A grieving husband had filed a suit stating that his wife died because of the microwaves delivered to her head from her cellular phone. As you can see, Motorola's stock lost 15 percent of its value in a few days on this news.

EXHIBIT 18.5 Motorola 1993

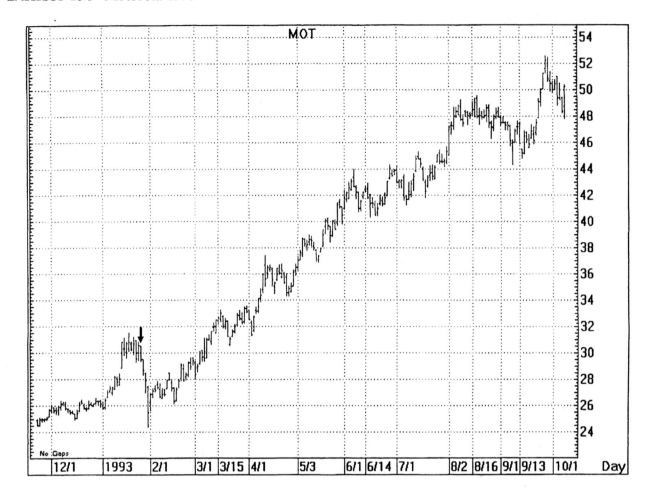

The biggest fear among investors during this period was the blockbuster story the television program "20/20" was supposed to air. As it turned out, the story was nothing but journalistic-hype. Motorola's stock rebounded and it proceeded to trade through its pre-event price of 29 1/2. Over the next 10 months, MOT became one of the best performers on the NYSE, appreciating over 60 percent.

LINDA:

I can't believe you trade a strategy that lasts more than a few days. This must really work.

LARRY:

It does and I wish it happened more often. When the occasion does arise, the potential profits are significant.

LINDA:

This strategy clearly points out why using your logic will get you into trouble.

LARRY:

Yes. It's logical to think a stock is going to drop in price on bad news. It becomes further reinforced when this news is exaggerated by the press. In these situations you must "let the market talk to you!"

LINDA:

What do you mean "talk to you?"

LARRY:

If the market is going up on bad news, it is telling you something. It's telling you it doesn't care about the bad news. It doesn't care about the problems. It's telling you it's going even higher.

LINDA:

Are your stops as tight with this strategy as they are in other strategies?

LARRY:

Not when I trade equities. Because I may be holding this position for weeks and even months, I give my stops some breathing room. This way, I can ride out the short-term corrections and stay in my position for as far as it takes me.

PART FOUR

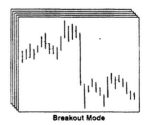

BREAKOUT MODE

CHAPTER **19**

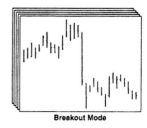
Breakout Mode

RANGE CONTRACTION

■ ■

Swing trading is profitable only when there are oscillations and good volatility. However, this volatility is quite cyclical in nature; the market experiences a constant ebb and flow of range contraction/range expansion. Toby Crabel elaborates on this principle in his book, *Day Trading with Short-Term Price Patterns and Opening Range Breakout*. He states that after the market has had a period of rest or range contraction, a trend day will often follow.

A trend day is one in which the market opens at one extreme of its range and closes at the other extreme. It covers a lot of distance with very few retracements and can initially "creep," picking up steam as the day progresses. Traders who come into the day unaware of the possibility of a trend day are usually caught trying to trade in a countertrend mode. As they scramble to cover losses in the late afternoon, the market may well tend to accelerate into the close.

How does one know when to jump on board a trending move? It is extremely difficult for the majority of traders to learn to switch gears from a "swing trading" style, looking for reactions and tests, to a "breakout mode" that calls for jumping on board the train. Many floor traders will make money 9 out of 10 days and then give half of it back trying to fight a trend day.

The first step is to learn to identify ahead of time the conditions which lead to a trend day. Label these days as "breakout mode" and then only trade them from a volatility-expansion system or a specific rule set.

This first pattern, ID/NR4, will explore one such rule set. It is a simple, effective entry combined with a resting stop. The whole key to trading this pattern is preidentifying the existing ID/NR4 condition.

An NR4 is a trading day with the narrowest daily range of the last four days. An inside day has a higher low than the previous day's low and a lower high than the previous day's high. Combining the two conditions sets up an ID/NR4 day.

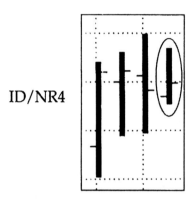

ID/NR4

Crabel's initial approach suggested a day-trading strategy following this setup. However, our research suggests that the trade should be held longer than one day.

In the breakout mode we can't predict the direction in which we are going to enter the trade. All we can do is predict that there should be an expansion in volatility. Therefore, we must place both a buy-stop and a sell-stop in the market at the same time. The price movement will then "pull us into" the trade.

Here are the rules:

1. Identify an ID/NR4.

2. The next day only, place a buy-stop one tick above and a sell-stop one tick below the ID/NR4 bar.

3. On entry day only, if we are filled on the buy side, enter an additional sell-stop one tick below the ID/NR4 bar. This means that if the trade is a loser, not only will we get stopped out with a loss, we will reverse and go short. (The rule is reversed if initially filled on the short side.)

4. Trail a stop to lock in accrued profits.

5. If the position is not profitable within two days and you have not been stopped out, exit the trade MOC (market on close.) Our experience has taught us that when the setup works, it is usually profitable immediately.

Here are a few examples.

EXHIBIT 19.1 S&P 500—December 1994

1. An ID/NR4 day. Tomorrow, we will place a buy-stop one tick above today's high and a sell-stop one tick below today's low.

2. We are filled on the sell side. A second buy-stop order is placed one tick above yesterday's high in case of a reversal.

3. This type of sell off is fairly rare (18 points in five trading sessions!), but they are the reason to trade this setup. This strategy gives you small gains and small losses, eventually producing a setup such as this one.

EXHIBIT 19.2 S&P 500—June 1995

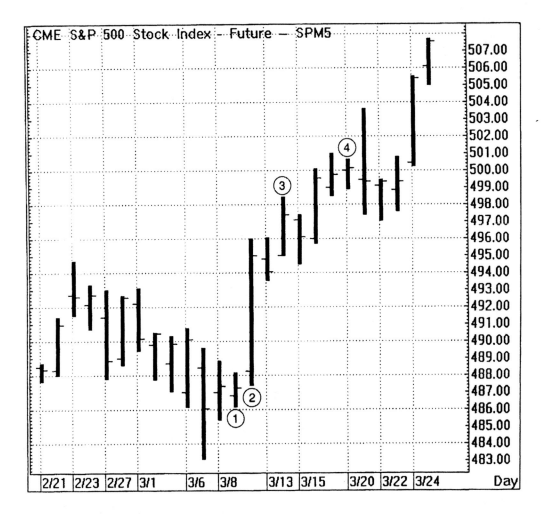

1. The range of the S&P bar on March 9, 1995, is the smallest range in four days and is an inside bar.

2. Our buy-stop is placed at 488.20 (one tick above the previous day's high) and is triggered on the opening at 488.50. The sell-stop placed at 486.10 (one tick below the previous day's low) is doubled in size in case of a reversal. As you can see, the market explodes, closing at 495.00, up 6.50 points from the opening. As this position becomes more profitable throughout the day, a trailing stop should be used to lock in the profit.

3. The market rises steadily over the next week. Our position has a healthy 10+ point profit, bringing us to another ID/NR4 setup on March 20. (For simplicity's sake, let's assume that we locked in our profits from March 10, 1995 and are flat.)

4. This type of setup happens from time to time and is a good example of what you can occasionally expect.

   - ID/NR4 setup

   - Buy-stop filled at 500.75

   - Sell-stop and reversal sell-stop filled at 498.90

   - Next day (two days after the setup) the market closes .45 points above our sell point. The position is closed out.

   - The loss from the March 20, 1995 setup is approximately 2.25 points plus slippage and commission.

If you trade this strategy and most other strategies in this manual, you must get used to this type of trade. As we mentioned in the previous example, this setup pattern often makes and loses small amounts of money, and occasionally you will get a trade that explodes, such as the one that occurred on March 10, 1995.

EXHIBIT 19.3 Abbot (ABT)—1995

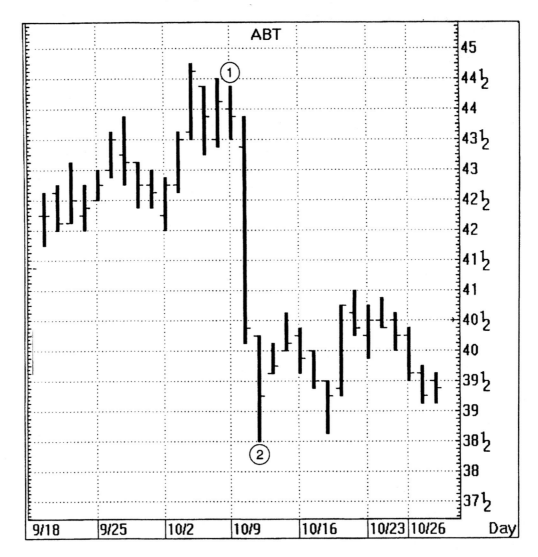

1. An NR4 inside day.
2. A sharp 10 percent two-day sell-off.

EXHIBIT 19.4 Natural Gas—February 1996

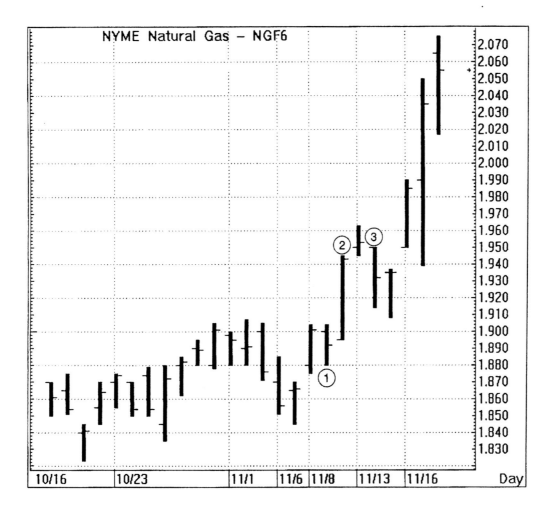

1. An NR4 inside day.

2. The breakout is to the upside. As you can see, the market opens on its low and closes on its high. You will often see this type of pattern from this setup.

3. A trailing stop will ensure locking in profits as the position corrects itself. Also, notice how the market rallies a few days later. Unfortunately, we will miss these occasional moves to assure capturing the one to four day profits.

LARRY:

The reason to trade this strategy is because the losses are small, and occasionally a big winner will fall into your lap.

LINDA:

The typical "GO FISH" strategy! Keep dropping your pole in the water and once in awhile you'll catch a big one.

LARRY:

Yes. It's also important for traders to realize the importance of stopping and reversing on a same-day whipsaw, because often that "big one" follows a "fakeout" losing trade.

LINDA:

It's amazing how sometimes the best trades occur after one group of market participants has been **trapped**. They'll later become fuel for the fire when their losses deepen. It definitely takes a certain amount of fortitude to trade breakouts.

LARRY:

Even if a trader chooses to skip trading patterns like these, it is vitally important to be aware of an initial low-volatility, range-contraction setup. At the very least, never try to trade against moves exploding out of these points. Better just to let the day go if you don't feel comfortable climbing on board.

LINDA:

That's true. Many novice traders misunderstand swing trading as a license to buy weakness or sell strength. When a trend day comes along, they get their head handed to them. It is a sucker play because the initial low volatility, creeping mode of a trend day lures people into thinking they can get by without a resting stop order in the marketplace. When the market starts to run away, it's natural to freeze up. Almost every trader has experienced this.

It is so important to identify the conditions when **not** to swing trade (i.e., low-volatility environments). Then we can work on **capturing** the breakout and learning how to jump on board this impulsive action.

LARRY:

What other patterns from Toby's book do you trade?

LINDA:

One of the simplest concepts which I use regularly is Toby's NR7. This represents the narrowest range of the last seven days. I automatically use this as a filter to switch to a breakout mode the day following an NR7. This means that I will not try to countertrend trade. Instead, I will try and enter the market in the direction it is moving.

CHAPTER **20**

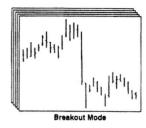
Breakout Mode

HISTORICAL VOLATILITY MEETS TOBY CRABEL

First, let's review historical volatility. It is simply a mathematical measurement of how much prices in a particular market fluctuate over a set period of time. The actual formula is provided in the Appendix, but it is also included as a study in many market software programs.

There are two interesting properties of volatility you should be aware of. The first is that it is quite cyclical—even more than price. The second is that it is more highly autocorrelated than price changes. What does this mean? Well, when volatility reverses direction, it is more likely to continue in that direction. Thus, once volatility starts to contract, it will continue to decrease until it reaches a critical reading. At this point, the cycle will reverse itself. Then when the volatility expands, the ensuing explosion will continue to propel the price in one direction.

We combine the historical volatility indicator with Toby Crabel's NR4 day or an inside-day pattern to identify these critical points. We have found this combination does a good job pinpointing explosive moves.

Here is the setup:

1. First, we will compare the six-day historical volatility reading to the 100-day historical volatility reading. We are looking for the 6/100 reading to be under 50 percent (in other words, for the six-day historical volatility reading to be less than one-half the 100 day historical volatility reading).

2. If rule one is met, today (day one) must be either an inside day or an NR4 day. When both rules one and two are met, we now have a setup.

3. On day two, place a buy-stop one tick above the day-one high and a sell-stop one tick below the day-one low.

4. If your buy-stop is filled, place an additional sell-stop one tick below the day-one low. (The reverse applies if your sell-stop is hit first.) This will allow you to reverse the position in case of a false breakout. This additional sell-stop is done on the entry day only, and expires on the close of this day. A trailing stop should be used to lock in profits on a winning trade.

Here are three examples from the bond market that occurred in late 1994 and early 1995.

EXHIBIT 20.1 Bonds—December 1994

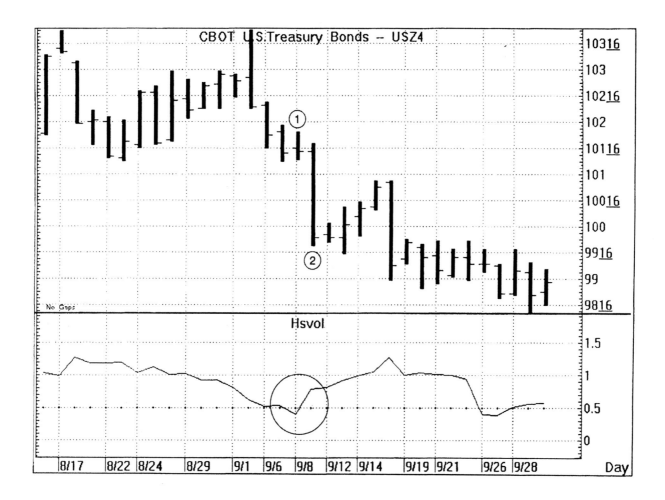

1. September 8, 1994, bonds have an inside day, an NR4, and a 6/100 day historical volatility reading under 50 percent.

2. A buy-stop is placed at 101-27, one tick above the day-one high, and a sell-stop is placed at 101-08, one tick below the day-one low. Our sell-stop is filled and a second buy-stop order is placed at 101-27. The market experiences a sharp sell-off and the bonds drop nearly a point and one-half for the day.

EXHIBIT 20.2 Bonds—June 1995

1. May 1, 1995, all the pieces are together again: an inside day, an NR4, and a 6/100 day historical volatility reading under 50 percent.

2. Bonds trade one tick above the day-one high of 105-13 and we are long.

3. Bonds move sharply higher and our protective sell-stop moves with the rise.

4. The Historical Volatility Meets Toby Crabel setup pattern identifies to the day the biggest weekly rally bonds have had in six years.

EXHIBIT 20.3 Bonds—March 1995

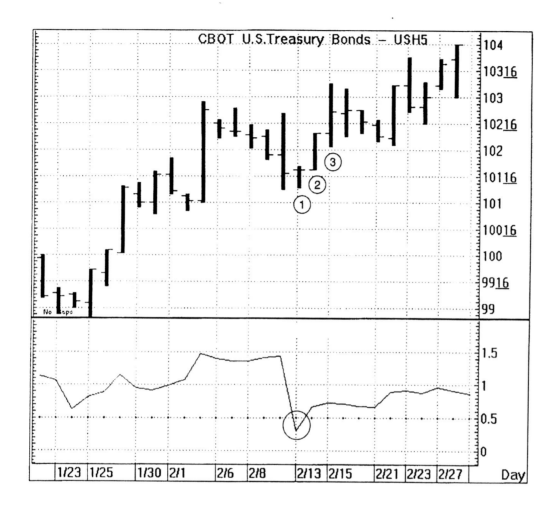

1. February 13, 1995, bonds experience an inside day and the 6/100 day historical volatility ratio is under 50 percent.

2. The next morning bonds open at 101-28 and we are long. An additional sell-stop order is placed at 101-08, one tick below the day-one low.

3. Bonds move on an intraday basis 44 ticks (over $1350/contract) higher.

166   Chapter 20

EXHIBIT 20.4 Micron Technology (MU)—1995

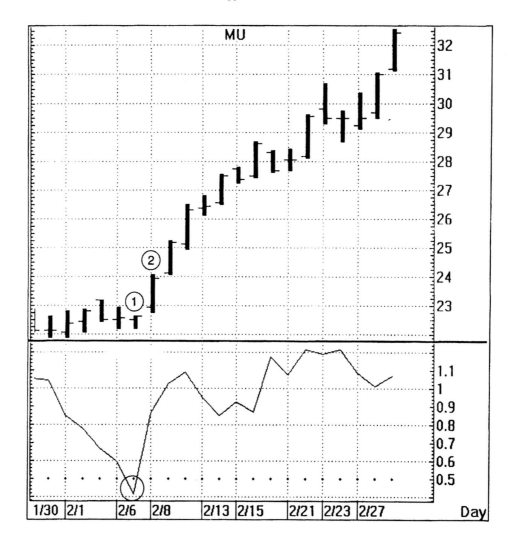

1. An NR4 and a 6/100 day historical volatility reading under 50 percent.

2. The market breaks to the upside and proceeds to appreciate over 20 percent in two weeks.

EXHIBIT 20.5 Crude Oil—January 1996

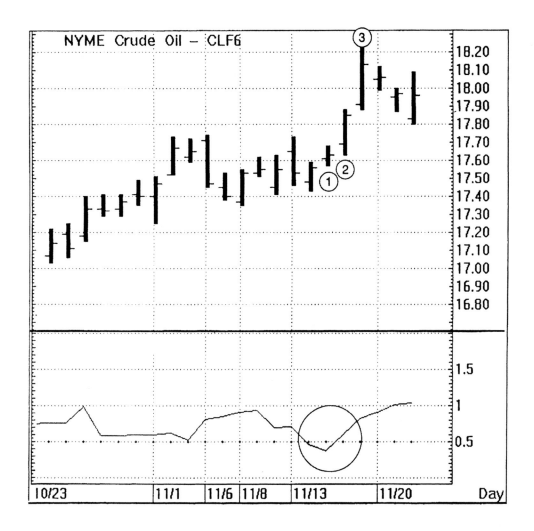

1. An NR4 combined with a 6/100 day historical volatility reading under 50 percent.

2. The market opens above the previous day's high and we are long.

3. Crude oil trades more than 50 cents above our previous day entry point.

EXHIBIT 20.6 Soybean Oil—December 1995

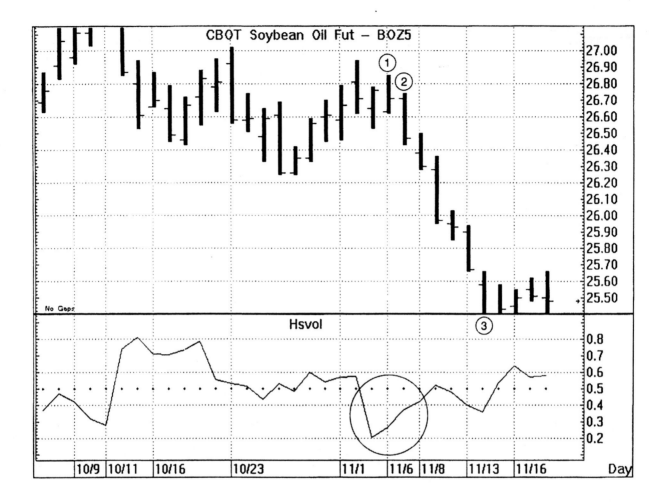

1. An NR4 combined with a 6/100 day historical volatility reading under 50 percent. Tomorrow, we will have a buy-stop one tick above today's high of 26.85 and a sell-stop one tick below today's low of 26.62.

2. Our sell-stop is triggered and we double our buy-stop at 26.86 in case the market reverses.

3. The market loses over 100 points in six trading sessions.

LINDA:

I love this strategy. Some powerful moves occur from these signals.

LARRY:

That's because it combines the best of two worlds. We are mathematically identifying periods of historically low volatility, and at the same time we are also identifying these same periods with pattern recognition.

LINDA:

Why do you use a 6/100 period for historical volatility? In your first book, you used a 10/100 day period.

LARRY:

The 6/100 day period helps identify short-term moves better than the 10-100 day period, which is more appropriate for intermediate-term moves.

LINDA:

So you are only looking for a very short-term move from this setup?

LARRY:

Yes. I will stay in the position as long as it continues to move in my favor. Usually though, I am out within one to four days.

PART FIVE

MARKET MUSINGS

CHAPTER 21

Market Musings

SMART MONEY INDICATORS

■ ■

LINDA:

These are some broader market indicators that I have used for trading the S&P and for monitoring the market in general. They are subjective tools and should always be used in conjunction with another indicator or pattern. However, I felt that specific enough guidelines could be given for their use and consequently you might find them useful.

SMART MONEY INDEX

The first indicator is called the "Smart Money Index." I came across it in *Barrons* in the mid-1980s. It was presented as a long-term indicator and it was used as a summation index to pinpoint long-term tops and bottoms by looking for divergences in the index against the price action in the Dow. I use the concept on a short-term basis in an entirely different way which we'll present to you here.

The smart money index is appropriate in a swing trading book if only to heighten a trader's awareness of weak hands (public speculative money) versus strong hands (smart, informed money), and the significance of morning reversals.

The general thesis is that weak hands (i.e., the public) tend to make emotional, uninformed decisions in the **first hour** of trading. The professionals represent the smart money and control the **last hour** of trading. The smart money index is comprised of the net change in the Dow for the first hour versus the net change in the Dow for the last hour.

Here is how you create the index.

1. Take the net change for the first hour in the Dow. Multiply it by –1. For example, if yesterday's close in the Dow was 4980 and after the first hour of trading today the Dow closes at 4985, it would have a net change of +5. Multiply this by –1 to get –5.

2. Take the net change for the last hour in the Dow and add it to the final number in rule 1. For example, if the Dow is at 4990 at 3:00 EST and closes the day at 4984 (4:00 EST), we add the last hour's net change of –6 to –5 for a total of –11 on the day.

3. A running summation index of the first hour (inverted) net change and the last hour's net change is logged.

Here are some more calculations to illustrate the Index's computation.

	1st Net Change	×	(–1)	+	Last hour change	=	Sum	Total
Day 1	10		–10	+	–2	=	–12	–12
Day 2	–5		5	+	–5	=	0	–12
Day 3	–20		20	+	10	=	30	18
Day 4	5		–5	+	20	=	15	33
Day 5	15		–15	+	–12	=	–27	6

You might want to look at the total summation index for historical purposes, but the only number that I use is the individual day's reading at the close. If the day's **sum** reading is greater than 20, look to be a buyer the next day. If the day's **sum** reading is less than 20, look to be a seller the next day. High readings usually accompany significant intermediate term reversals in the stock market. On average, four to five signals will be given per month.

It really pays to be conscious of how a market trades in the last hour. Again, if you are long and the market closes firm, carry your position home overnight. There are overwhelming odds that the market will follow-through the next morning. Also, be especially on guard against making emotional mistakes in the first hour of trading. This applies not only to the S&Ps but to all markets. You don't want to get trapped by an early morning reversal.

TICK INDICATOR

This next indicator is used only for trading the S&Ps. I'm sure many traders are already familiar with it. For those who are not, the tick represents the difference between all the stocks listed on the New York Stock Exchange that are on upticks verses all the stocks trading on downticks. A chart of the tick can almost function as an overbought/oversold indicator. In this case we are going to look for tick divergences.

There are several reasons why this pattern is included in this book. The first is that it again illustrates the important concept of a test. In this particular case it also includes a nonconfirmation, or principle of divergence. Second, far too many people try to overtrade the S&P. We know of countless traders who make money in the morning and give it back in the afternoon. It is far more important to concentrate on a few choice strategies than to try to capture every move. (Greed will absolutely be one's undoing in the S&P market.)

Third, if a trader did nothing but concentrate on this one pattern, he or she would be able to make a living trading. It takes patience though to wait for just one setup!

BUY SETUP (SELLS ARE REVERSED)

1. The S&P must make a morning low where the ticks give a reading of less than −350 (minus 350).

2. The S&P then must make an equal or lower low in price at least 90 minutes later. The tick must make a higher low than it did the first time. (Even five ticks higher is sufficient for this pattern.) If the ticks improve from this second low point by 100 ticks, we will enter at-the-market. A protective sell-stop is then entered at the low of the day.

3. Trail a stop to protect any accrued profits. I usually like to protect at least 50 percent of any equity gained (e.g., if the market rallies two points, move the stop up to lock in at least one point.)

Chapter 21

4. You may hold a winning trade overnight and take profits on follow-through the next morning. In the S&P it is usually best to be very defensive with any quick gains. A trailing stop will often close out the trade before the end of the day.

Study the examples and then paper trade this pattern first. You should notice that the more volatility the market has, the better this trade will set up. It is **critical** to have a resting stop in the market after you have entered a trade. The best trades will show a profit right away!

On October 5, the S&P makes a lower low while the tick makes a higher low. When the tick rallies back by 100, this confirms the end of the downtrend. We buy the S&P at-the-market and place a stop beneath the recent low. The market rallies another 4 points.

EXHIBIT 21.1 S&P—5-Minute

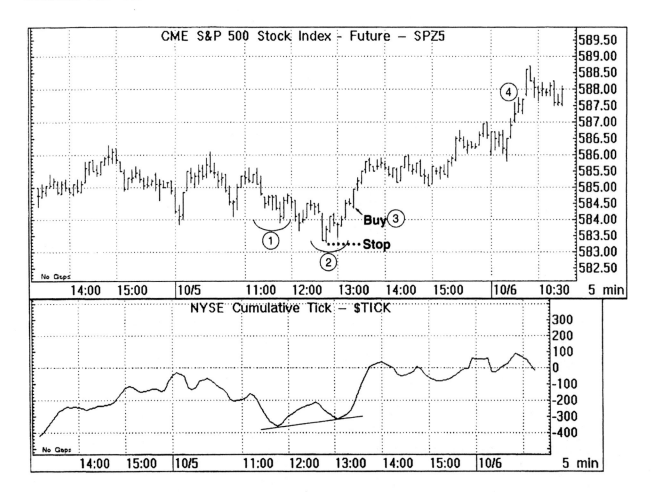

EXHIBIT 21.2 S&P—5-Minute

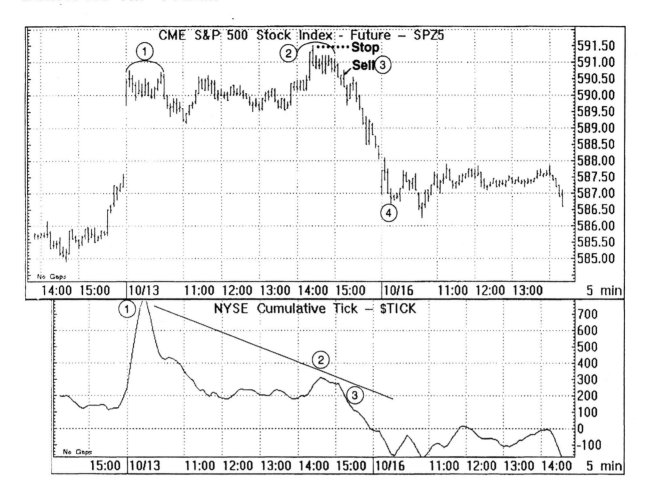

The market makes a higher high while the tick makes a lower high. When the tick sells off by 100, we sell the S&P at-the-market and place a stop above the recent high. The market sells off another three points. (Notice how the S&P formed a fakeout shakeout pattern leading to the sell-off.)

It is also useful to be aware of any extreme intraday readings—high or low—in the tick, even if no divergence sets up. This information can help you anticipate a trade for the **next** day (the day after the high reading). For example, when a majority of stocks are on an uptick, and the market is able to register an intraday reading of greater than 400, this represents strong buying power. Everyone is buying! What happens the next day when nobody is left to buy?

If day one registers a reading of ticks greater than 400, then on day two we will look to short a morning rally. If day one registers a reading of lower than –400, then on day two we will look to buy a morning pullback. Please remember to always use stops when entering on a reversal in the S&P. This pattern will not serve you particularly well in an extremely strong trending market. However, I used it throughout the bull market rally of 1995, and it worked quite well. It is also useful to watch the tick on an hourly chart. Look for two to three consecutive +/–400 readings over one to two days to set up a reversal.

The main trick to successful S&P trading using this type of pattern is to look for 5-minute or 30-minute Turtle-Soup patterns on the bar chart. You must have the patience to wait for the **test** and not try to pick a bottom or top!

EXHIBIT 21.3 $SPX and Tick—60 Minute

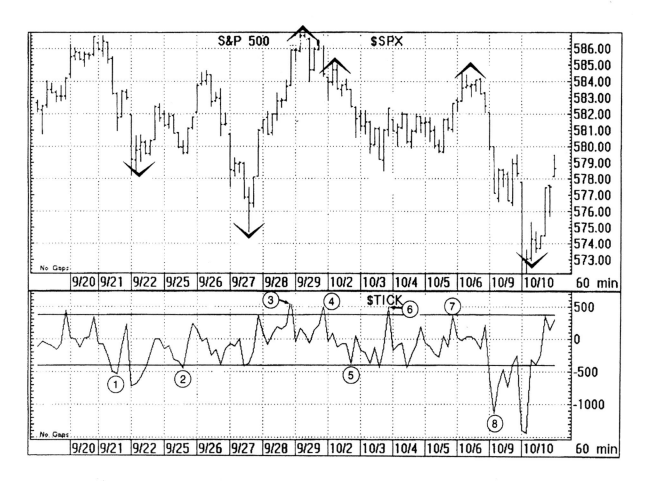

When the tick reaches a reading of greater than 400 or less than −400, we will anticipate the market making an intraday reversal the next day. It usually presents a significant trading opportunity.

EXHIBIT 21.4 $SPX and Tick

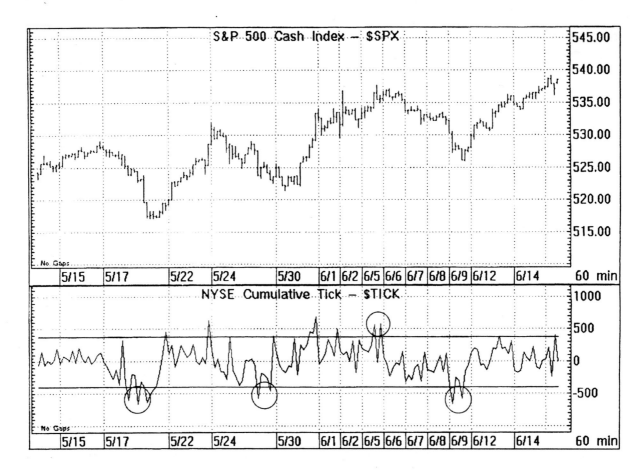

Clusters of tick readings that are greater than 400 or less than –400 warn of potential intermedate-term reversals.

ARMS INDEX

The last indicator we would like to mention is the Arms Index, originally known as the TRIN, or Trading Index.

This is a ratio of two ratios: advances/declines divided by up-volume/down-volume. It is a standard transmission on all data-feed services. We will use a five-day moving average of the Arms Index. A reading greater than 1.20 indicates a potential intermediate-term bottom or oversold condition. A reading less than .80 indicates a potential short-term top or overbought condition. These are short-term trading opportunities only (one to three days).

As with any overbought/oversold indicator, the Arms Index can give premature signals in a strongly trending market. We have found the buy signals to be more reliable than the sell signals. (This could be due to an obvious upside bias over the last 15 years.)

Lots of professionals have kept either a 5- or 10-day moving average of this indicator at some time or another. Many consider it part of their daily routine to log this number at night along with moving averages of the advance/decline line (which helps monitor the market's breadth).

Study the examples and then determine for yourself if it would be of service to you. We have found it to be particularly helpful when trading equities. The best trades come when there is a confluence of signals from several indicators which all point in the same direction.

182   Chapter 21

EXHIBIT 21.5   TRIN

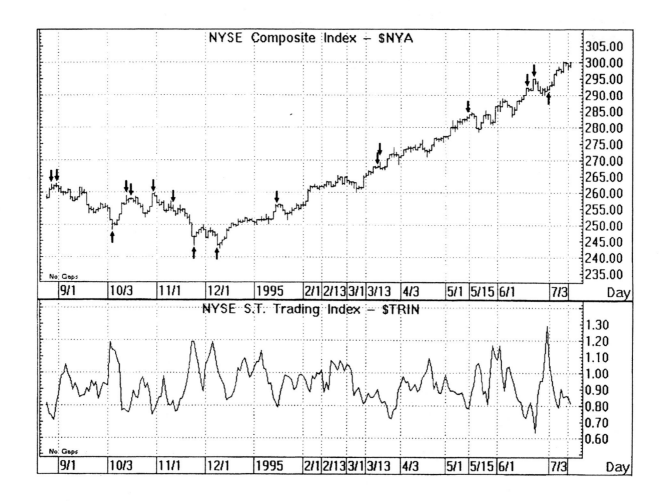

The arrows mark the places where the five-day moving average of the TRIN hit a reading of greater than 1.20 (buy) or less than .80 (sell).

CHAPTER **22**

MORE WORDS ON TRADE MANAGEMENT

"Trust also your own judgment, for it is your most reliable counselor. A man's mind has sometimes a way of telling him more than seven watchmen posted on a high tower."

Ecclesiasticus

Now that you have seen our trading strategies, let us share a few more lessons we've learned over the years.

First, if you are a beginning trader, only paper trade initially. Enter each trade in a ledger exactly as if you were trading with real dollars. You must take it seriously! Only after you have a legitimate record should you trade an actual account.

You will realize that most of your profits are small and you will probably be disappointed. However, most of the losses will be small, too, and this is the way trading usual ends up. **Your first goal in trading should be to become a breakeven trader.**

With time and practice, the losses will become smaller and might even become scratches (no loss at all). With luck and experience, there will also be a small handful of large trades in a month. In this respect, trading is strictly a game of preservation of capital. Then one gets lucky once in awhile, and everyone should realize by now that luck is the residue of effort!

Many beginning traders feel overwhelmed by looking at too many technical indicators. As the old saying goes, if you give a person one watch, they'll know what time it is. If you give that person two watches, they'll never be certain what time it is! Most of the time, oscillators and moving averages are not going to all line up at once for the perfect trade. Approach the market in tiny bite-sized pieces and it will be more manageable. Much of the time, even professionals don't have a clear picture of what is going on, but they have learned to have the patience to wait for select, specific setups. You must learn to trade on only the most recognizable and reliable patterns.

You must also learn to watch for the signals that the market itself gives you. Notice what it is telling you when it has shallow reactions. If it doesn't want to go down, the next move up should be very strong. It is also important to note its response to bullish or bearish news.

- **Your own preconceived opinions about where the market might go will be your biggest enemy.** The opinions of friends or brokers will be your next biggest enemy.

- **Don't carry losing positions overnight!** This one piece of advice will save you thousands of dollars. It is far better to exit and try entering at a more favorable level the next day.

- **Correct mistakes immediately!** If the market is closed and you realize you made a mistake, get out on the next day's **opening**. Don't try to trade out of it. The odds are that a losing position will get **worse** as the day goes on!

- **If the market offers you a windfall profit on a trade, you must lock it in!** This means either take profits or trail an extremely tight stop on any balance. It is vitally important to be defensive and not give back profits when swing trading.

The lower your expectations, the happier you will be. Be pleasantly surprised when a windfall occurs, but never be looking for "the big one." The market will decide how much profit to give you. **Only you** can decide how much to limit your loss.

It's not unusual for beginners to give up all control to the markets. They wait for the market to give them a profit. They wait for a loss to occur so they know when to get out. Their profits and losses can be said to be determined by the market itself.

More seasoned traders know that while the markets do indeed give profits when they're agile enough to grab them, they (the traders themselves) determine their losses. Your only control over the markets, your best control over your profitability, lies in determining your risk, that is, how much **you** decide to lose when a trade turns against you.

The trader who masters this one, single concept will have taken the biggest step we know toward consistent profitability.

Lastly, take these patterns and make them your own. Create your own variations; take our ideas and modify them. These concepts will provide a good, solid foundation, but ultimately experience will be your best teacher.

LINDA:

I think by now we've harped enough about money management. What is one more thing that contributes to a trader's success?

LARRY:

Consistency. It's the only way to know if what you do works or if it doesn't work. If you are constantly tweaking indicators, you'll never learn whether they work or not. Most of the patterns in this book are conceptually simple.

LINDA:

Yes! We are both firm believers in the K.I.S.S philosophy (Keep it simple, stupid.) Much of trading really comes down to having the mental fortitude to grind it out.

LARRY:

I think some people have the misconception that professional traders make money every day. Everyone feels that he or she is the only one who is not making money.

LINDA:

No way. Professionals can have high and dry times, too! Even floor traders can go weeks without being profitable. You just have to step back and ask, "How much did I **lose** during these periods?"

LARRY:

That's why I say a person's first goal should be to become a break-even trader. If you wait for good setups and follow the rules, it usually doesn't take long for a winning trade to make back a string of losses.

LINDA:

It's very analogous to playing poker. The real discipline is in waiting for the right hands. You don't have to play every hand but you must bet very aggressively when you have the best hand. Don't bet money when the odds are not fully in your favor!

CHAPTER 23

Market Musings

BE PREPARED!

■ ■

The importance of doing your homework the night before to prepare for the next day's trading cannot be emphasized enough! The whole object of swing trading is to anticipate setups so that we are not in a reactive mode the next day. Spontaneous trades are not a good way to make a living! Just as the professional athlete must have a game plan, so must the professional trader. Have you ever noticed how many athletes have a pregame routine they go through? Routines and rituals keep us in a steady frame of mind. They help us to focus solely on the task at hand—in this case, the next day's trading opportunities.

When we started comparing notes on how we prepare for the next day's trades, we discovered that we do basically the same thing. We do our homework in the evening (which takes some planning considering we both have families), and also we both keep lots of notebooks!

We thought it would be interesting and educational for you to see our thought processes on preparing for the day.

LINDA:

I guess I'm fortunate to have had some good role models when I first started in the business because by nature I tend to procrastinate. If I haven't prepared for the next day, it's easy for me to feel overwhelmed, and I'll tend not to make any trades at all. I've pretty much adopted the routine of two people I worked for in the early 80s. I'm sure I wouldn't be successful today without this discipline.

The first person I worked for had a routine of logging numbers such as closing prices and the 10-day moving average of the Arms Index, advance/declines, put-call ratios, etc. He also updated a book of charts published by Security Market Research each night. This service had an oscillator which was also plotted by hand. The routine took 45 minutes and was done every night. The next morning, the charts were studied on the hour-long BART train ride into San Francisco, when any interesting buy or sell setups were written out. Once in the city, another hour was spent checking the previous day's trades and writing out new stock orders. This person started out as a floor trader in the equity options in 1978 and is still a professional trader today.

The second person I worked for was also a floor trader in the equity options. He would be at work 1 1/2 hours before the market opened and would stay for two hours after the close. What would he do? Update charts by hand, draw trend lines, study the day's trades he had made, look over all the trades I had made and comment on them (UGH), write out his trading cards for the next day, enter his exit orders before the opening to take advantage of any opening gaps in his favor, scan the exchanges for any undervalued out-of-the-money call options that other traders might have forgotten about . . . you know, I think I could write a whole book just on this person's routine. The point is, he was one of the least conspicuous traders on the floor but he was probably one of the most profitable. And guess what? . . . He's still down on the trading floor today. He was adamant about following a particular methodology. I never really saw him deviate from his personal style of trading.

My first boss made a living selling option premium and my second boss made his living buying it. Yet both were consistent in their particular trading style. I'll never forget the saying of my second boss: "Trading is a business like any other business. Learn to buy wholesale and sell retail. If they don't come for your inventory, mark it down and move it out the door" (This is called taking a loss, by the way.)

From my first mentor I adopted a routine of logging the numbers every day. I have the same information on my computers, but it doesn't mean anything to me unless I write it down by hand. I have notebooks full of numbers, stored in my basement, which I'll never look at again. But they are my proof that I did my homework every night. This was the first similarity with Larry that I noticed—notebook-itis.

LARRY:

I write down every trade I make in addition to my daily P&L. I know how much I have made or lost each day. I've also kept every notebook.

LINDA:

When did you start keeping notebooks?

LARRY:

When I decided to become a professional trader. It has now become a habit.

LINDA:

Do you keep any type of daily worksheet?

LARRY:

I keep a special one for the S&P's. I also write down any special setups in the futures for the next day—and I'll also write down the daily high and low of a market. Then I program this information into my Bloomberg terminal. I also get a daily printout from TradeStation of any setups, but truthfully, I like walking through each market individually and looking for setups on the charts. It is more tedious but it gives me a better feel for the markets.

LINDA:

Do you do this with the equity markets in addition to the futures markets?

LARRY:

Yes, I do; I follow about 100 equities. I also scan for news both at night and in the morning.

LINDA:

That's a lot of information to process.

LARRY:

Well, I try to narrow the information down to the setups I believe have the most potential. If I have too many things to look at I feel scattered.

LINDA:

Same here. I'll note all the setups the night before on a worksheet but I might only end up making one to three trades the next day. Either things don't set up quite right, or I don't like the way the market opens. I miss a lot of trades, too. It's better to follow fewer markets and make one good trade than to get sloppy and disorganized. It's like poker. Don't make the bet unless the hand sets up just right.

LARRY:

The Patience Game . . . Do you write down your trades?

LINDA:

Absolutely. Writing down your trades is the best exercise in the world. I write down the date and time I entered the trade, buy/sell, quantity, contract, and fill price. The log remains open until I close out the trade, at which time I enter the exit date and price. Only then do I calculate the profit or loss. Needless to say, when you have a nasty losing trade, it really sticks out. There's also good incentive to lock in winners because then you can actually record the profit in your log.

I have to share a little story with you. It is an excellent habit to write down your equity every day, which I do. However, I allowed myself to become impressed with new account highs . . . oh, in April 1988. Kiss of Death! What a jinx on my account! It was impossible to make money after that. Now I start each month at zero and track it only for the month.

LARRY:

Euphoria is an absolute enemy. My friend who is a **market wizard** said that he started off his year each January at **zero** and would build it up from there.

LINDA:

Actually, that's a very common practice among floor traders. The people I worked for went beyond that. Each month they would actually draw any profits out of the account to bring it back down to a certain level. They figured that if there weren't any profits in the account, they couldn't lose them!

LARRY:

You know, I have to comment on something you brought up earlier. It was when you were talking about how you have to go about your routine each day, grinding out trades, and then two or three times a month you get the perfect trade and have a windfall. This is exactly what happens with me. I originally thought I was lucky and that being a good trader had nothing to do with it. Now I know better.

LINDA:

That's right. The good traders are the ones who can hold their ground the majority of the month and participate in that small handful of trades that are windfalls. The real skill is in not **losing** money!

CHAPTER 24

FINAL THOUGHTS

When we decided to create this manual, our goal was to write a book that presented strategies in a simple and concise manner. We hope we have achieved our goal and we hope you enjoyed reading this manual as much as we enjoyed writing it.

We believe that successful trading does not have to be complicated. The strategies taught to you in this manual identify times when the odds favor a move in one direction. By having the patience to wait for those setups you will have an edge over the many traders who "shoot from the hip."

By now, we are sure you are aware of how we feel about money management. In our opinion, none of the strategies in this book work without the rigid use of stops. In accordance with this, we would like to end this manual with a research study done by a friend of ours, Fernando Diz, a finance professor at Syracuse University. His work reveals the reasons why Commodity Trading Advisors (CTAs) succeed and fail. Professor Diz's research comes to one conclusion: money management is the real secret to trading success.

CHAPTER **25**

THE SECRETS OF SUCCESSFUL TRADING

by Fernando Diz[1]

A question that is often asked by anyone aspiring to be a trader is: What makes a trader successful?

Anyone who has read Jack Schwager's two *Market Wizards* books will know that there are at least three components to successful trading: the trader's psychological makeup, the trading system's edge, and strict money management. Although knowing about these provide you with very useful general guidelines, any trader aspiring to be successful could benefit from a more systematic study of traders' successes and, more important, failures. With this purpose in mind, I conducted a study of 925 CTA programs over the 1974–1995 period.[2] Since I am not a psychologist,

---

[1] Fernando Diz is an assistant professor of finance at Syracuse University School of Management.

[2] The data used in study was provided by the Barclay Trading Group. Special thanks to Sol Waksman and Peter Nicols for their helpful comments.

I only focused on the last two components of successful trading: the edge and money management. The purpose of the study was to find out how the edge and money management affect a program's success.[3]

The definition of success in this study was very simple: a CTA or program was successful if it was able to stay in business. Of the 925 CTAs or programs studied between 1974 and 1995, 490 are still in business while the remaining 435 went out of business.

The "edge" of a program was proxied by five different and complementary measures:

- Monthly compounded return—bottom line performance of a program or trader.

- Maximum monthly return—return on the most successful month. Proxy for the program's return potential and whether it is trading at optimal levels.

- Sharpe Ratio—measure of returns per unit of standard deviation. Allows you compare returns of programs with different volatility.

- Skewness of returns—a positive number tells you that the program has a tendency to generate returns higher than the mean more often than normal.

- Kurtosis of returns—measures how returns are packed around the mean relative to a normal distribution. A positive number tells you that there is higher probability of finding returns near the mean compared to a normal distribution.

The first one is the monthly compounded rate of return over the life of the program. This measures the level of returns that the program has been able to yield over its life. To give you an idea of the range of returns that you can find among different programs over their lives, the maximum monthly return was 10.36 percent and the minimum monthly return was –6.04 percent. The second measure of the edge was the return on the most successful month. This measure focuses on the magnitude of

---

[3] Diz, Fernando (1995), *CTA Survival and Return Distribution Characteristics*, working paper, Syracuse University.

potential gains and gives you an idea of the magnitude of the program's edge and whether the program is trading at optimal levels or not. The program with the most successful month had a return of 319 percent while the program with the smallest most successful month had a return of 0.8 percent. The third measure used was the Sharpe ratio. This is a measure of returns per unit of risk. It allows you to compare returns from programs with very different risk characteristics. Suppose that you have two programs A and B that have the same monthly compounded return, but program A has a Sharpe ratio that is two times as large as that of program B. What this means is that program A can generate the same returns as program B but with half the risk or volatility. The last two measures of the edge, skewness and kurtosis, are rather technical and give you an idea of how capable a program has been in generating larger returns with a high degree of probability.

Just as edge measures increases in a CTA's equity curve, money management looks at the dips and recoveries in that curve.

The quality of the program's money management was proxied by five different measures:

- Standard deviation of returns—consistency with which programs achieve their returns. Gives you an idea of what kind of drawdowns and large returns to expect.

- Maximum monthly drawdown—magnitude of potential loses. Gives you an idea of risk controls and whether the program trades at optimal levels or not.

- Months to recover from worst drawdown—other things equal, programs with good money management will recover quicker than programs with poor money management.

- Standard deviation of times to recover from drawdown—measures the consistency with which programs come out of drawdowns.

- Time to recover from worst drawdown as a percent of the program's life—indicates how much of a program's business life was spent recovering from the worst drawdown.

The first one was the standard deviation of monthly returns. The standard deviation gives you an idea of the probability of big hits or large drawdowns relative to the program's average monthly return. The second measure of money management was the maximum monthly drawdown. This measure focuses on the magnitude of potential losses and gives you an idea of both risk controls and whether the program is trading at optimal levels or not. To give you a better idea of the magnitude of drawdowns that you can find, the largest drawdown was 81 percent, while the smallest drawdown was no drawdown at all. The average monthly drawdown for all programs studied was 16 percent. Although looking at any single monthly drawdown is important, perhaps even more important is the amount of time that it takes a program to come out of a loss. For example, suppose that a program's initial equity is $1,000,000 and that in the next month the program experiences a 25 percent drawdown, reducing its equity to $750,000. What is the maximum number of months that would take the program to bring the equity back to $1,000,000? This is what the third money management variable measures. It took 137 months for the worst program in this category to recover from its worst drawdown. It is not surprising that after failing to recover from its worst drawdown in more than 11 years, this program went out of business. It took an average of 20 months for the average program to recover from its worst drawdown. This measure is important because it can be theoretically shown that a program with good money management can recover from drawdowns much faster than a program with poor money management. What does this mean? It means that if you look at two traders that have the same edge (system), the one with better money management will recover from drawdowns faster. What if one trader has a larger edge than the other? If both traders use good money management, the one with the larger edge is likely to recover faster from drawdowns. So much for the academic explanation. What is more likely to happen out there?

I have looked at the most successful trend-follower traders out there and found that their distribution of monthly returns is remarkably similar; they have a comparable edge. The big difference between them is in their losses. *The traders with the highest average returns have consistently smaller losses*. This is an example of money management improving your existing edge.

The fourth money management variable measures the consistency with which programs recover from drawdowns. A large number for this measure means that programs do not recover consistently from their losses over time. This is probably related to both the edge of the program and its money management alike. The last money management variable measures the longest time that a program spent recovering from a drawdown expressed as a fraction of the program's life. For example, if a program had been in business for 24 months and it spent 12 months recovering from its worst drawdown the value of this variable would be 0.5. This variable tries to capture the importance of a program's worst drawdown relative to the time that it has been in business.

The results of the study show that both the edge and money management strongly affect CTAs likelihood of success. This general result only confirms what *The Market Wizards* had suggested. But my interest was much more specific than that. I wanted to know if there were important differences between the successful (survivors) and the unsuccessful (out of business) CTAs or programs. First, I looked at their edge. You can see the results in Exhibit 25.1.

Two things definitely stand out from looking at the results in Exhibit 25.1. Successful programs were able to yield a monthly compounded rate of return 48 percent higher than unsuccessful programs.

EXHIBIT 25.1 Average Values for the "Edge" Variables for Successful and Unsuccessful Programs

"Edge" Variable	Successful Programs	Unsuccessful Programs
Monthly compounded return %	1.35%	0.91%
Maximum monthly return %	30.80	34.70
Sharpe ratio	15.91	9.89

More importantly, not only were they able to generate larger returns for their clients but they did so with lower risk than the unsuccessful programs. The average Sharpe ratio for successful programs was 61 percent larger than the one for unsuccessful programs. The ability to generate larger returns with lower risk leads us to the second component of successful trading: money management. The results of a similar comparison are shown in Exhibit 25.2.

EXHIBIT 25.2 Average Values for Money Management Variables for Successful and Unsuccessful Programs

Money Management Var.	Successful Programs	Unsuccessful Programs
Standard deviation of returns	8.09%	9.10%
Maximum monthly drawdown	15.30%	17.80%
Months recovering from worst drawdown	19	22
Variability in drawdown recovery in months	6	7
Time recovering from worst drawdown as percent of program life	0.32	0.41

The results in Exhibit 25.2 are quite revealing. Successful programs' returns are 11 percent less variable than those of their unsuccessful counterparts. Furthermore, successful traders experience lower maximum drawdowns, they recover from drawdowns faster, and they are more consistent in doing so. Finally, notice that unsuccessful programs spend a larger proportion of their business life recovering from their worst drawdown!

The lesson from these results is clear: successful traders have a larger edge and much better money management than unsuccessful traders. Remember that these are average differences between successful and unsuccessful programs. These results do not tell you however, which one of these two components might be more important in explaining success. This is exactly the question that I wanted to answer. The question that I asked myself was: If I had to explain success with only one, or two variables, which ones would give me the most explanatory power for discriminating between successful and unsuccessful traders? As you will see, the results were rather astounding.

If I had to explain success with only one variable, the one that predicted success or failure most accurately was the amount of time a program spent recovering from its worst drawdown as a percentage of its life.

Very small values of this variable were associated with success, and very large values predicted failure. An important lesson to be drawn from this finding that is particularly suited to traders who have been in business for a very short time is: *Avoid large drawdowns and recover from them quickly if you want to stay in business (but do not increase risk to do it!)*. More interestingly, when you include the maximum number of months that it takes a trader to recover from its worst drawdown in the analysis, these two variables alone explained 88 percent of the predictive power of a model with all the edge and money management variables put together! This clearly demonstrates that although unsuccessful traders have a smaller edge over successful ones, their smaller edge is not the cause of their failure; their money management is! In fact, their smaller edge may very well be a result of poor money management. This is quite revealing. What it basically tells us is that most CTAs or programs that have gone out of business had enough of an edge to stay in business! **The cause of their failure can be traced to poor money management**.

Two of the most important components of successful trading are the edge of a system and sound money management. This study confirms this notion. Successful traders have a larger edge and better money management than unsuccessful traders. Unlike popular belief however, this study shows that the smaller edge of unsuccessful traders is not the cause of their failure. Traders failure can be explained almost exclusively by their poor money management practices.

The techniques taught in this book will give you the trading edge you need. If you want to increase this edge, the importance of money management cannot be stressed enough.

APPENDIX

HISTORICAL VOLATILITY CALCULATIONS

The historical volatility is defined as the standard deviation of the logarithmic price changes measured at regular intervals of time. Since settlement prices are usually considered the most reliable, the most common method of computing volatility involves using settlement-to-settlement price changes. We defined each price change, x_i, as:

$$x_i = \ln(P_i / P_{i-1})$$

where P_i is the price of the underlying contract at the end of the ith time interval.

P_i/P_{i-1} is sometimes referred to as the *price relative*.

Week	Underlying Price	$\ln(P_i/P_{i-1})$	Mean	Deviation from Mean	Deviation Squared
0	101.35				
1	102.26	+.008939		.007771	.000060
2	99.07	−.031692		−.032859	.001080
3	100.39	+.013236		.012069	.000146
4	100.76	+.003679		.002512	.000006
5	103.59	+.027699	+.001167	.026532	.000704
6	99.26	−.042698		−.043865	.001924
7	98.28	−.009922		−.011089	.000123
8	99.98	+.017150		.015982	.000255
9	103.78	+.037303		.036136	.001306
10	102.54	−.012020		−.013188	.000174
		+.011674			.005778

We first calculate the standard deviation of the logarithmic price changes:

$$\text{standard deviation} = \sqrt{.005778/9}$$
$$= \sqrt{.000642}$$
$$= .025338$$

We then calculate the annual volatility by multiplying the standard deviation by the square root of the time interval between price changes. Since we looked at price changes every week, the time interval is 365/7:

$$\text{annualized volatility} = .025338 \times \sqrt{(365/7)}$$
$$= .025338 \times \sqrt{52.14}$$
$$= .025338 \times 7.22$$
$$= .1829 \ (18.29\%)$$

Reprinted from: Nathanberg, Sheldon. *Option Volatility & Pricing, Advanced Trading Strategies and Techniques*, 2d ed., (Chicago: Probus Publishing, 1994), Appendix B.

MOORE RESEARCH CENTER—STATISTICAL STUDIES

Please read this paragraph before examining the following tables! We wish to be perfectly clear that we are not testing mechanical systems. Rather, we are examining a variable to see if there is a tendency that might be useful as part of an entry or exit methodology. Your eye might initially be drawn to the column reading "average net." This is not meant to imply any level of profitability. We are more concerned with the percentages to see if a market goes up or down more in response to an initial condition. We are also testing to see if an indicator has uniform behavior across all markets.

The following text will help you better understand how to read the tables.

Introduction

Moore Research Center of Eugene, Oregon, has provided statistical testing to supplement our own research efforts. These studies highlight certain market tendencies and serve as a way to quantify characteristics of market behavior. The tests also provide such information as frequency of pattern occurrence, directional bias, and daily bar characteristics. We use this statistical testing for its comparative value only. It is not meant to represent a mechanical system. Thus, no statistics such as commissions or slippage are factored in, nor are data on total profitability or maximum drawdown provided.

We will present a short description of each test and comment on the results. Before we continue, though, it is important to mention the testing methodology. The tests are run on actual contract data which are rolled from the lead contract to the next front month either one day before first notice day, or five days before expiration (whichever comes first). We run the buy and sell tests independently to examine the potential for directional bias.

Since we are looking for tendencies or probabilities, sample size is important. The tests are run on 10 years of data across 25 markets. The number of days examined is listed in the column labeled "Total Days." The total number of occurrences tested can be calculated by dividing the number of wins by the percentage of wins. For example, 48(60%) indicates that there were 48 positive results with a "win/loss" ratio of 60%. 48/.6 = 80 total occurrences.

We also like to see if a pattern or relationship holds true across multiple markets. This builds our confidence that the pattern represents a true principle of market behavior. Most of the studies are run on just one to two variables. We feel that these results are robust and that the relationships should hold true in the future. We also hope that you can use these tests as a **departure point** in your own system development or examination of market behavior.

Daily Bar Statistical Profiles

This first set of studies profiles a market's price action following a day that has closed at the extreme of its range. The tests show a tendency for an intraday reversal following this condition. This pattern forms a basis for the 80-20's bar strategy discussed in Chapter 6.

We will describe each column on the studies so that you can examine the results for yourself. First is a column listing the total number of days tested. This is followed by a listing titled "Setup Days." Here, the frequency of occurrence is shown. The next column profiles the percentage of time that the market opened up or down. After this, we can see the number of times that the market penetrated the previous day's high or low and the average amount of the penetration. Finally, the study shows the percentage of time that the market closed up or down.

Let's look at the first analysis titled "Historical Upper 90%." This study profiles the market's action following a day where the market closed in the upper 10 percent of its range. If we look at the S&Ps, we can see that this setup occurred 17 percent of the time across 2436 days. The next morning the market opened up 48 percent of the time. It then penetrated the previous day's high 85 percent of the time by an average amount of 2.00 points. Lastly, it closed up only 50 percent of the time.

If we look at the next study, it profiles the market's action following days closing in the upper 20 percent of the range. As you can see, the results are just about the same. This same tendency towards mid-day reversal also holds true for markets closing in the lower extreme of their range—in fact, even more so. When the S&Ps closed in the lower 20 percent of their range, there was only a 42 percent probability that they would close lower the following day.

It is also interesting to note that despite the upside bias to the S&Ps and the bonds over the last 10 years, the penetrations through the previous days extremes tended to be significantly deeper on the sell side.

The last set of studies in this section profiles the day following a WR7, which is the **widest** range of the last seven days. We examined both WR7s with a high close and WR7s with a low close. The probabilities for the majority of markets favored a close in the opposite direction the following day. Sugar was an extreme example. It closed in the opposite direction 60 percent of the time. These tests would indicate that it is definitely a good idea to take profits on a range expansion bar (in other words, one with a very wide range). They also suggest that the WR7 day could be a useful pattern to combine with 80-20's bars.

EXHIBIT A.1 Historical Upper 90% Statistics

Historical Upper 90% Statistics
LBRMoore TRADING, INC.

Mkt	Contracts	Total Days	Setup Days	Opened Up	Penetrated High	Average Penetration	Closed Up
SP	86H-95M	2436	408(17%)	194(48%)	348(85%)	2.00	196(48%)
YX	86H-95M	2436	458(19%)	196(43%)	377(82%)	1.14	215(47%)
USAM	86H-95M	2431	418(17%)	218(52%)	336(80%)	0.58	207(50%)
ED	86H-95M	2439	192(8%)	86(45%)	145(76%)	0.05	83(43%)
SF	86H-95M	2439	263(11%)	111(42%)	175(67%)	0.52	125(48%)
DM	86H-95M	2439	277(11%)	143(52%)	208(75%)	0.35	143(52%)
BP	86H-95M	2439	255(10%)	117(46%)	173(68%)	0.94	119(47%)
JY	86H-95M	2438	318(13%)	149(47%)	215(68%)	0.49	164(52%)
GC	86G-95M	2443	253(10%)	119(47%)	191(75%)	2.67	93(37%)
SI	86H-95N	2458	237(10%)	103(43%)	192(81%)	8.72	105(44%)
HG	86H-95N	2458	394(16%)	202(51%)	291(74%)	1.54	198(50%)
CL	86G-95N	2496	402(16%)	217(54%)	352(88%)	0.27	191(48%)
HO	86G-95N	2495	305(12%)	162(53%)	251(82%)	1.07	162(53%)
NG	92G-95V	984	123(12%)	77(63%)	108(88%)	0.036	59(48%)
KC	86H-95U	2493	336(13%)	173(51%)	279(83%)	2.30	152(45%)
CC	86H-95U	2490	252(10%)	110(44%)	199(79%)	18	105(42%)
SB	86H-95V	2548	444(17%)	167(38%)	324(73%)	0.17	179(40%)
JO	86F-95U	2525	415(16%)	207(50%)	311(75%)	1.79	197(47%)
W	86H-95U	2509	395(16%)	201(51%)	326(83%)	3.62	205(52%)
C	86H-95U	2509	342(14%)	171(50%)	270(79%)	2.70	149(44%)
S	86F-95U	2552	341(13%)	162(48%)	266(78%)	6.44	149(44%)
CT	86H-95V	2519	489(19%)	269(55%)	408(83%)	0.92	252(52%)
LC	86G-95V	2549	377(15%)	186(49%)	319(85%)	0.48	200(53%)
PB	86G-96G	2640	398(15%)	247(62%)	336(84%)	1.08	207(52%)
LH	86G-95V	2557	308(12%)	150(49%)	243(79%)	0.55	156(51%)

EXHIBIT A.2 Historical Upper 80% Statistics

Historical Upper 80% Statistics
LBRMoore TRADING, INC.

Mkt	Contracts	Total Days	Setup Days	Opened Up	Penetrated High	Average Penetration	Closed Up
SP	86H-95M	2436	720(30%)	354(49%)	577(80%)	2.06	357(50%)
YX	86H-95M	2436	746(31%)	317(42%)	579(78%)	1.14	351(47%)
USAM	86H-95M	2431	698(29%)	376(54%)	554(79%)	0.54	352(50%)
ED	86H-95M	2439	457(19%)	227(50%)	336(74%)	0.06	211(46%)
SF	86H-95M	2439	575(24%)	255(44%)	383(67%)	0.48	275(48%)
DM	86H-95M	2439	589(24%)	283(48%)	403(68%)	0.35	289(49%)
BP	86H-95M	2439	580(24%)	273(47%)	381(66%)	0.96	279(48%)
JY	86H-95M	2438	606(25%)	273(45%)	375(62%)	0.49	282(47%)
GC	86G-95M	2443	509(21%)	247(49%)	357(70%)	2.66	206(40%)
SI	86H-95N	2458	470(19%)	203(43%)	349(74%)	7.92	197(42%)
HG	86H-95N	2458	641(26%)	316(49%)	452(71%)	1.34	301(47%)
CL	86G-95N	2496	697(28%)	370(53%)	579(83%)	0.27	337(48%)
HO	86G-95N	2495	616(25%)	336(55%)	481(78%)	0.90	312(51%)
NG	92G-95V	984	234(24%)	138(59%)	191(82%)	0.035	116(50%)
KC	86H-95U	2493	613(25%)	310(51%)	478(78%)	2.11	279(46%)
CC	86H-95U	2490	533(21%)	222(42%)	390(73%)	18	235(44%)
SB	86H-95V	2548	711(28%)	263(37%)	478(67%)	0.17	279(39%)
JO	86F-95U	2525	679(27%)	337(50%)	500(74%)	1.68	336(49%)
W	86H-95U	2509	685(27%)	338(49%)	536(78%)	3.53	342(50%)
C	86H-95U	2509	675(27%)	326(48%)	506(75%)	2.40	320(47%)
S	86F-95U	2552	635(25%)	297(47%)	465(73%)	5.89	281(44%)
CT	86H-95V	2519	738(29%)	386(52%)	578(78%)	0.85	366(50%)
LC	86G-95V	2549	685(27%)	330(48%)	547(80%)	0.44	360(53%)
PB	86G-96G	2640	622(24%)	345(55%)	497(80%)	0.98	306(49%)
LH	86G-95V	2557	633(25%)	292(46%)	480(76%)	0.49	311(49%)

EXHIBIT A.3 Historical Lower 10% Statistics

Historical Lower 10% Statistics
LBRMoore TRADING, INC.

Mkt	Contracts	Total Days	Setup Days	Opened Down	Penetrated Low	Average Penetration	Closed Down
SP	86H-95M	2436	215(9%)	88(41%)	190(88%)	3.05	93(43%)
YX	86H-95M	2436	212(9%)	106(50%)	174(82%)	1.74	88(42%)
USAM	86H-95M	2431	271(11%)	118(44%)	215(79%)	0.55	116(43%)
ED	86H-95M	2439	180(7%)	66(37%)	134(74%)	0.05	70(39%)
SF	86H-95M	2439	211(9%)	100(47%)	144(68%)	0.49	97(46%)
DM	86H-95M	2439	208(9%)	99(48%)	146(70%)	0.36	92(44%)
BP	86H-95M	2439	184(8%)	87(47%)	119(65%)	1.23	82(45%)
JY	86H-95M	2438	256(11%)	122(48%)	166(65%)	0.45	114(45%)
GC	86G-95M	2443	187(8%)	100(53%)	144(77%)	3.12	81(43%)
SI	86H-95N	2458	243(10%)	134(55%)	185(76%)	9.12	112(46%)
HG	86H-95N	2458	381(16%)	186(49%)	257(67%)	1.34	167(44%)
CL	86G-95N	2496	343(14%)	193(56%)	292(85%)	0.34	179(52%)
HO	86G-95N	2495	339(14%)	178(53%)	268(79%)	0.96	160(47%)
NG	92G-95V	984	126(13%)	99(79%)	108(86%)	0.033	63(50%)
KC	86H-95U	2493	357(14%)	226(63%)	291(82%)	2.29	186(52%)
CC	86H-95U	2490	335(13%)	179(53%)	249(74%)	21	176(53%)
SB	86H-95V	2548	340(13%)	173(51%)	249(73%)	0.16	120(35%)
JO	86F-95U	2525	356(14%)	208(58%)	295(83%)	1.86	174(49%)
W	86H-95U	2509	343(14%)	219(64%)	292(85%)	3.68	178(52%)
C	86H-95U	2509	298(12%)	191(64%)	259(87%)	2.67	158(53%)
S	86F-95U	2552	426(17%)	237(56%)	351(82%)	6.10	187(44%)
CT	86H-95V	2519	383(15%)	241(63%)	334(87%)	0.91	207(54%)
LC	86G-95V	2549	315(12%)	148(47%)	266(84%)	0.45	139(44%)
PB	86G-96G	2640	439(17%)	249(57%)	391(89%)	1.02	243(55%)
LH	86G-95V	2557	275(11%)	156(57%)	226(82%)	0.55	130(47%)

EXHIBIT A.4 Historical Lower 20% Statistics

Historical Lower 20% Statistics
LBRMoore TRADING, INC.

Mkt	Contracts	Total Days	Setup Days	Opened Down	Penetrated Low	Average Penetration	Closed Down
SP	86H-95M	2436	375(15%)	176(47%)	312(83%)	2.79	156(42%)
YX	86H-95M	2436	402(17%)	194(48%)	310(77%)	1.48	161(40%)
USAM	86H-95M	2431	533(22%)	243(46%)	395(74%)	0.52	234(44%)
ED	86H-95M	2439	427(18%)	193(45%)	315(74%)	0.05	183(43%)
SF	86H-95M	2439	498(20%)	240(48%)	323(65%)	0.44	223(45%)
DM	86H-95M	2439	489(20%)	236(48%)	328(67%)	0.34	213(44%)
BP	86H-95M	2439	438(18%)	209(48%)	278(63%)	1.08	186(42%)
JY	86H-95M	2438	560(23%)	259(46%)	339(61%)	0.41	252(45%)
GC	86G-95M	2443	426(17%)	235(55%)	296(69%)	2.73	172(40%)
SI	86H-95N	2458	539(22%)	291(54%)	391(73%)	7.65	234(43%)
HG	86H-95N	2458	626(25%)	306(49%)	415(66%)	1.25	273(44%)
CL	86G-95N	2496	640(26%)	358(56%)	513(80%)	0.32	326(51%)
HO	86G-95N	2495	665(27%)	362(54%)	508(76%)	0.88	329(49%)
NG	92G-95V	984	243(25%)	178(73%)	196(81%)	0.033	123(51%)
KC	86H-95U	2493	626(25%)	393(63%)	495(79%)	2.31	321(51%)
CC	86H-95U	2490	654(26%)	358(55%)	467(71%)	19	322(49%)
SB	86H-95V	2548	626(25%)	314(50%)	442(71%)	0.16	240(38%)
JO	86F-95U	2525	584(23%)	327(56%)	445(76%)	1.74	276(47%)
W	86H-95U	2509	628(25%)	404(64%)	514(82%)	3.55	326(52%)
C	86H-95U	2509	702(28%)	439(63%)	587(84%)	2.31	378(54%)
S	86F-95U	2552	711(28%)	364(51%)	538(76%)	5.93	316(44%)
CT	86H-95V	2519	614(24%)	369(60%)	502(82%)	0.84	317(52%)
LC	86G-95V	2549	586(23%)	279(48%)	465(79%)	0.46	278(47%)
PB	86G-96G	2641	707(27%)	364(51%)	582(82%)	0.91	369(52%)
LH	86G-95V	2557	528(21%)	280(53%)	406(77%)	0.51	245(46%)

EXHIBIT A.5 Historical WR7 and Higher-Close Statistics

Historical WR7 and Higher-Close Statistics
LBRMoore TRADING, INC.

Mkt	Contracts	Total Days	Setup Days	Opened Up	Penetrated High	Average Penetration	Closed Up
SP	86H-95M	2436	143(6%)	69(48%)	106(74%)	2.05	77(54%)
YX	86H-95M	2436	142(6%)	60(42%)	98(69%)	1.11	69(49%)
USAM	86H-95M	2431	174(7%)	83(48%)	111(64%)	0.47	80(46%)
ED	86H-95M	2439	185(8%)	93(50%)	97(52%)	0.08	85(46%)
SF	86H-95M	2439	190(8%)	92(48%)	110(58%)	0.55	101(53%)
DM	86H-95M	2439	182(7%)	88(48%)	107(59%)	0.38	95(52%)
BP	86H-95M	2439	164(7%)	80(49%)	92(56%)	1.02	83(51%)
JY	86H-95M	2438	174(7%)	78(45%)	81(47%)	0.45	79(45%)
GC	86G-95M	2443	167(7%)	74(44%)	79(47%)	3.23	63(38%)
SI	86H-95N	2458	161(7%)	59(37%)	80(50%)	7.58	60(37%)
HG	86H-95N	2458	184(7%)	94(51%)	123(67%)	1.29	88(48%)
CL	86G-95N	2496	199(8%)	103(52%)	140(70%)	0.35	100(50%)
HO	86G-95N	2495	199(8%)	109(55%)	135(68%)	0.93	104(52%)
NG	92G-95V	984	85(9%)	42(49%)	60(71%)	0.037	42(49%)
KC	86H-95U	2493	168(7%)	81(48%)	108(64%)	2.16	80(48%)
CC	86H-95U	2490	171(7%)	74(43%)	102(60%)	19	80(47%)
SB	86H-95V	2548	189(7%)	62(33%)	102(54%)	0.19	75(40%)
JO	86F-95U	2525	177(7%)	77(44%)	92(52%)	1.92	82(46%)
W	86H-95U	2509	172(7%)	79(46%)	114(66%)	4.01	85(49%)
C	86H-95U	2509	178(7%)	71(40%)	92(52%)	2.41	85(48%)
S	86F-95U	2552	175(7%)	69(39%)	89(51%)	5.58	67(38%)
CT	86H-95V	2519	194(8%)	92(47%)	125(64%)	0.74	96(49%)
LC	86G-95V	2549	156(6%)	64(41%)	98(63%)	0.40	70(45%)
PB	86G-96G	2641	190(7%)	93(49%)	110(58%)	0.95	87(46%)
LH	86G-95V	2557	164(6%)	72(44%)	104(63%)	0.41	71(43%)

EXHIBIT A.6 Historical WR7 and Lower-Close Statistics

Historical WR7 and Lower-Close Statistics (LBRMoore Trading, Inc.)

Mkt	Contracts	Total Days	Setup Days	Opened Down	Penetrated Low	Average Penetration	Closed Down
SP	86H-95M	2436	174(7%)	78(45%)	119(68%)	3.32	79(45%)
YX	86H-95M	2436	180(7%)	83(46%)	115(64%)	1.89	79(44%)
USAM	86H-95M	2431	136(6%)	60(44%)	95(70%)	0.55	62(46%)
ED	86H-95M	2439	126(5%)	66(52%)	82(65%)	0.05	68(54%)
SF	86H-95M	2439	157(6%)	82(52%)	93(59%)	0.40	70(45%)
DM	86H-95M	2439	162(7%)	80(49%)	97(60%)	0.34	75(46%)
BP	86H-95M	2439	158(6%)	87(55%)	84(53%)	1.12	76(48%)
JY	86H-95M	2438	158(6%)	70(44%)	65(41%)	0.54	56(35%)
GC	86G-95M	2443	171(7%)	87(51%)	67(39%)	2.60	70(41%)
SI	86H-95N	2458	152(6%)	90(59%)	90(59%)	11.04	80(53%)
HG	86H-95N	2458	140(6%)	74(53%)	87(62%)	1.38	64(46%)
CL	86G-95N	2496	186(7%)	91(49%)	139(75%)	0.29	96(52%)
HO	86G-95N	2495	164(7%)	71(43%)	104(63%)	0.83	69(42%)
NG	92G-95V	984	70(7%)	54(77%)	46(66%)	0.037	31(44%)
KC	86H-95U	2493	192(8%)	97(51%)	119(62%)	2.32	95(49%)
CC	86H-95U	2490	155(6%)	81(52%)	96(62%)	20	79(51%)
SB	86H-95V	2548	165(6%)	72(44%)	77(47%)	0.20	68(41%)
JO	86F-95U	2525	170(7%)	94(55%)	108(64%)	1.55	77(45%)
W	86H-95U	2509	153(6%)	87(57%)	99(65%)	3.79	80(52%)
C	86H-95U	2509	149(6%)	88(59%)	99(66%)	2.58	81(54%)
S	86F-95U	2552	160(6%)	67(42%)	101(63%)	4.33	76(48%)
CT	86H-95V	2519	181(7%)	101(56%)	119(66%)	0.89	82(45%)
LC	86G-95V	2549	183(7%)	78(43%)	120(66%)	0.45	83(45%)
PB	86G-96G	2641	171(6%)	86(50%)	137(80%)	0.80	88(51%)
LH	86G-95V	2557	164(6%)	83(51%)	116(71%)	0.51	81(49%)

Historical ROC Reports

This study examines the indicator used for part of the momentum pinball strategy. A three-period RSI is run on a one-period rate of change. If the reading is greater than 70, the next day's opening is sold. If the reading is less than 30, the next day's opening is bought. We then examine the initial entry at the following morning's open and the following day's close. No protective stops are used. Our main intent is to examine the difference between the setup day's opening and the following day's opening. We are looking for evidence to support our theory that this ROC/RSI indicator has some value as a short-term overbought/oversold study to help capture Taylor's swing trading rhythm. We definitely feel that there is enough of a tendency displayed by this indicator that other people might be interested in examining it for their own system development.

This set of studies is run off daily bars only. It is not meant to be a representation of the complete momentum pinball strategy that employs a first hour range breakout.

EXHIBIT A.7 Historical ROCRSI Buy Report

LBRMoore TRADING, INC. — *Historical ROCRSI Buy (70, 30) Report*

Enter on: Open

	Futures Data		Exit on Next Open				Exit on Next Close			
Future	Contracts	Total Days	Win(%)	Avg Net	Avg Profit	Avg Loss	Win(%)	Avg Net	Avg Profit	Avg Loss
SP	86H-95U	2500	140(52%)	148	1311	-1095	143(53%)	211	1793	-1556
YX	86H-95U	2499	138(54%)	110	738	-631	145(57%)	142	948	-920
USAM	86H-95U	2495	137(51%)	46	521	-455	129(48%)	-3	650	-614
ED	86H-95U	2503	135(55%)	9	119	-123	131(53%)	0	149	-169
SF	86H-95U	2503	135(58%)	67	580	-647	135(58%)	81	712	-797
DM	86H-95U	2503	136(58%)	42	410	-474	122(52%)	23	543	-549
BP	86H-95U	2503	156(61%)	118	612	-653	148(58%)	86	745	-818
JY	86H-95U	2502	132(57%)	98	563	-528	137(60%)	100	614	-657
GC	86G-95V	2528	143(63%)	28	197	-257	126(55%)	13	271	-305
SI	86H-95U	2501	150(58%)	22	307	-367	147(57%)	5	358	-454
HG	86H-95U	2501	146(61%)	69	307	-308	151(63%)	95	353	-352
CL	86G-95V	2562	160(61%)	56	267	-271	149(57%)	77	388	-330
HO	86G-95V	2560	129(51%)	-30	309	-376	132(52%)	-21	433	-507
NG	92G-95V	984	65(62%)	134	417	-339	63(61%)	205	597	-397
KC	86H-95U	2493	171(65%)	240	760	-727	151(57%)	267	1120	-883
CC	86H-95U	2490	143(54%)	1	176	-207	151(57%)	37	234	-229
SB	86H-95V	2548	144(60%)	41	191	-183	158(66%)	49	215	-268
JO	86F-95U	2525	135(53%)	30	282	-250	144(56%)	45	357	-352
W	86H-95U	2509	161(56%)	9	161	-187	150(52%)	30	248	-211
C	86H-95U	2509	148(56%)	0	104	-130	148(56%)	-1	133	-168
S	86F-95U	2552	155(60%)	32	266	-313	142(55%)	24	347	-364
CT	86H-95V	2519	144(55%)	73	462	-401	150(57%)	126	595	-501
LC	86G-95V	2549	151(58%)	32	178	-169	147(56%)	44	249	-221
PB	86G-96G	2639	128(53%)	12	318	-332	122(50%)	6	417	-411
LH	86G-95V	2557	151(61%)	38	177	-182	149(60%)	53	224	-206

EXHIBIT A.8 Historical ROCRSI Sell Report

Historical ROCRSI Sell (70, 30) Report
LBRMoore TRADING, INC.

Enter on: Open

Futures Data			Exit on Next Open				Exit on Next Close			
Future	Contracts	Total Days	Win(%)	Avg Net	Avg Profit	Avg Loss	Win(%)	Avg Net	Avg Profit	Avg Loss
SP	86H-95U	2500	124(49%)	-123	973	-1177	105(42%)	-269	1391	-1446
YX	86H-95U	2499	138(53%)	5	494	-553	110(42%)	-100	708	-696
USAM	86H-95U	2495	120(48%)	33	538	-440	109(44%)	-41	651	-583
ED	86H-95U	2503	151(57%)	9	106	-123	141(54%)	9	141	-143
SF	86H-95U	2503	146(58%)	103	541	-506	139(55%)	48	596	-633
DM	86H-95U	2503	136(55%)	46	422	-407	119(48%)	-2	510	-470
BP	86H-95U	2503	115(51%)	69	614	-497	113(50%)	34	691	-624
JY	86H-95U	2502	140(57%)	67	544	-558	128(52%)	-1	591	-638
GC	86G-95V	2528	159(65%)	60	207	-211	136(56%)	22	236	-243
SI	86H-95U	2501	141(63%)	47	300	-383	116(52%)	-10	385	-434
HG	86H-95U	2501	133(53%)	4	284	-317	117(47%)	-6	371	-341
CL	86G-95V	2562	150(60%)	53	323	-343	135(54%)	35	377	-361
HO	86G-95V	2560	158(56%)	-11	392	-533	141(50%)	-55	473	-590
NG	92G-95V	984	63(55%)	117	466	-314	55(48%)	28	501	-414
KC	86H-95U	2493	148(61%)	178	820	-821	119(49%)	60	1055	-895
CC	86H-95U	2490	163(62%)	33	178	-208	156(60%)	40	235	-250
SB	86H-95V	2548	160(63%)	44	168	-170	141(56%)	-1	189	-240
JO	86F-95U	2525	143(52%)	21	245	-225	158(58%)	11	278	-356
W	86H-95U	2509	156(54%)	11	187	-195	135(47%)	6	259	-215
C	86H-95U	2509	179(61%)	25	118	-120	169(57%)	28	147	-132
S	86F-95U	2552	126(56%)	46	278	-247	115(51%)	43	395	-322
CT	86H-95V	2519	148(54%)	29	370	-371	146(53%)	18	459	-485
LC	86G-95V	2549	121(49%)	-4	177	-175	123(49%)	12	248	-219
PB	86G-96G	2639	161(58%)	66	401	-392	158(57%)	54	472	-492
LH	86G-95V	2557	141(56%)	30	202	-190	137(55%)	40	254	-217

2-Period Rate of Change Studies

This study examines entries taken on the **close** of a reversal in the 2-period rate of change. It then looks at exiting on the next day's opening and the next day's close. We can see that the trade opens in our favor a large percentage of the time for both buy and sell entries across the majority of markets. It also closes in our favor the majority of the time.

This is impressive considering that a buy signal is given, on average, one out of every four days—and likewise with sell signals. The percentages hold up across all markets!

On the Fresh Sell report, it is particularly interesting to note the high percentage of times that natural gas, coffee, and the grain markets open in your favor.

Please remember that the study is examining probabilities and tendencies only. **This is not meant to be a mechanical system.** However, it does demonstrate that this indicator might also be used to help capture Taylor's three-day rhythm.

EXHIBIT A.9 Historical Fresh ROC Buy Report

LBRMoore TRADING, INC. — Historical Fresh ROC Buy Report

Enter on: Close

	Futures Data		Exit on Next Open				Exit on Next Close			
Future	Contracts	Total Days	Win(%)	Avg Net	Avg Profit	Avg Loss	Win(%)	Avg Net	Avg Profit	Avg Loss
SP	86H-95U	2500	339(57%)	83	475	-435	340(57%)	168	1135	-1117
YX	86H-95U	2499	309(51%)	19	280	-253	337(56%)	75	623	-616
USAM	86H-95U	2495	370(62%)	53	237	-246	326(55%)	47	495	-493
ED	86H-95U	2503	402(70%)	16	51	-67	369(64%)	16	92	-119
SF	86H-95U	2503	337(53%)	27	354	-337	339(53%)	39	540	-528
DM	86H-95U	2503	333(53%)	9	256	-269	335(53%)	31	415	-408
BP	86H-95U	2503	326(52%)	27	373	-352	333(53%)	51	557	-527
JY	86H-95U	2502	331(54%)	49	384	-341	333(54%)	73	536	-472
GC	86G-95V	2528	326(51%)	-4	115	-126	304(47%)	-10	213	-211
SI	86H-95U	2501	329(51%)	1	139	-144	312(49%)	-13	273	-285
HG	86H-95U	2501	352(56%)	15	164	-176	316(50%)	35	332	-267
CL	86G-95V	2562	377(61%)	30	142	-145	328(53%)	41	314	-268
HO	86G-95V	2560	339(53%)	35	208	-163	345(54%)	27	341	-348
NG	92G-95V	984	131(52%)	-31	130	-206	121(48%)	-16	368	-371
KC	86H-95U	2493	311(50%)	-22	340	-378	318(51%)	-56	650	-781
CC	86H-95U	2490	300(49%)	-17	73	-101	316(51%)	-7	165	-187
SB	86H-95V	2548	342(53%)	2	77	-81	352(54%)	15	185	-185
JO	86F-95U	2525	358(57%)	15	99	-98	335(54%)	33	236	-203
W	86H-95U	2509	368(62%)	17	63	-58	342(57%)	26	176	-176
C	86H-95U	2509	357(60%)	11	51	-49	335(57%)	7	98	-111
S	86F-95U	2552	343(54%)	19	137	-118	326(51%)	-6	245	-268
CT	86H-95V	2519	356(59%)	36	166	-151	336(56%)	73	381	-316
LC	86G-95V	2549	362(57%)	4	67	-77	346(54%)	13	179	-182
PB	86G-96G	2638	374(58%)	26	132	-121	320(50%)	7	357	-342
LH	86G-95V	2557	411(64%)	19	71	-75	363(57%)	31	179	-162

EXHIBIT A.10 Historical Fresh ROC Sell Report

Historical Fresh ROC Sell Report
LBRMoore TRADING, INC.

Enter on: Close

Futures Data			Exit on Next Open				Exit on Next Close			
Future	Contracts	Total Days	Win(%)	Avg Net	Avg Profit	Avg Loss	Win(%)	Avg Net	Avg Profit	Avg Loss
SP	86H-95U	2500	325(54%)	42	408	-393	298(50%)	-66	1031	-1155
YX	86H-95U	2499	350(58%)	53	253	-219	305(50%)	-51	545	-651
USAM	86H-95U	2495	325(54%)	26	235	-224	293(49%)	16	498	-449
ED	86H-95U	2503	383(66%)	15	55	-65	344(60%)	10	103	-126
SF	86H-95U	2503	369(59%)	59	321	-315	311(50%)	3	540	-524
DM	86H-95U	2503	355(57%)	52	265	-232	305(49%)	1	423	-406
BP	86H-95U	2503	336(54%)	47	365	-331	303(49%)	-14	538	-543
JY	86H-95U	2502	325(53%)	13	354	-369	316(51%)	5	493	-511
GC	86G-95V	2528	389(60%)	35	141	-123	332(51%)	11	235	-225
SI	86H-95U	2501	384(60%)	25	137	-145	309(49%)	-20	296	-319
HG	86H-95U	2501	355(57%)	42	196	-164	325(52%)	18	303	-295
CL	86G-95V	2562	381(61%)	30	152	-161	319(51%)	19	301	-275
HO	86G-95V	2560	363(58%)	17	194	-227	316(50%)	1	341	-347
NG	92G-95V	984	179(69%)	87	192	-151	132(51%)	-18	309	-362
KC	86H-95U	2493	404(65%)	146	430	-376	323(52%)	50	746	-697
CC	86H-95U	2490	365(59%)	28	105	-86	337(55%)	22	189	-181
SB	86H-95V	2548	411(63%)	24	82	-76	330(51%)	0	185	-191
JO	86F-95U	2525	387(63%)	39	117	-92	312(51%)	22	247	-207
W	86H-95U	2509	423(70%)	25	62	-61	325(54%)	18	171	-160
C	86H-95U	2509	408(69%)	13	44	-57	325(55%)	14	111	-104
S	86F-95U	2552	381(60%)	23	117	-116	320(50%)	8	279	-264
CT	86H-95V	2519	365(61%)	80	214	-130	316(53%)	46	372	-320
LC	86G-95V	2549	369(58%)	4	65	-81	313(49%)	-5	179	-185
PB	86G-96G	2638	390(60%)	40	147	-123	337(52%)	39	366	-320
LH	86G-95V	2557	414(65%)	20	78	-89	341(54%)	9	186	-196

14-Period ADX Table

This table reveals the percentage of the time in which the 14-period ADX spends in a certain range for each future. For example, the S&P has an ADX value of between 30 and 39 for 17 percent of the time, and 7 percent of the time, it has an ADX value of between 40 and 49. Under the column labeled "trend," it should come as no surprise that the ADX has a positive slope for almost half of the time. The last column on the chart lists the average value for the ADX, which tends to be approximately 25. Usually, the best trading markets occur when the ADX has a value of 25 or greater. It does not necessarily matter if the slope is negative or positive. What is most important is that the market has volatility in addition to good average daily range.

We thought it was interesting to note that the statistics were fairly uniform across all of the markets. On average, the ADX will have a value of 30 or greater 28 percent of the time.

EXHIBIT A.11 Futures 14-Period ADX Statistics

Futures ADX:14 Statistics

Futures Data			Trend	Range Data						
Future	Contracts	Days	Times(%)	0-9(%)	10-19(%)	20-29(%)	30-39(%)	40-49(%)	50-59(%)	Avg
S & P 500(CME)	86H-95U	2500	1135(45%)	52(2%)	1074(43%)	762(30%)	414(17%)	165(7%)	29(1%)	24
NYSE Composite(NYFE)	86H-95U	2643	1205(46%)	46(2%)	1085(41%)	811(31%)	503(19%)	165(6%)	27(1%)	24
30-Year T-Bonds(CBT)	86H-95U	2674	1319(49%)	16(1%)	844(32%)	937(35%)	495(19%)	300(11%)	72(3%)	27
Eurodollars(IMM)	86H-95U	2671	1328(50%)	10(0%)	724(27%)	947(35%)	545(20%)	324(12%)	107(4%)	28
Swiss Franc(IMM)	86H-95U	2658	1294(49%)	44(2%)	919(35%)	962(36%)	542(20%)	168(6%)	23(1%)	25
Deutsche Mark(IMM)	86H-95U	2671	1287(48%)	42(2%)	867(32%)	978(37%)	556(21%)	162(6%)	66(2%)	26
British Pound(IMM)	86H-95U	2665	1257(47%)	44(2%)	993(37%)	955(36%)	431(16%)	173(6%)	43(2%)	25
Japanese Yen(IMM)	86H-95U	2649	1229(46%)	75(3%)	869(33%)	886(33%)	463(17%)	241(9%)	97(4%)	26
Gold(CMX)	86G-95V	2707	1266(47%)	63(2%)	1102(41%)	936(35%)	396(15%)	145(5%)	56(2%)	24
Silver(CMX)	86H-95U	2661	1219(46%)	83(3%)	1078(41%)	1025(39%)	337(13%)	84(3%)	45(2%)	23
Copper(CMX)	86H-95U	2661	1260(47%)	18(1%)	893(34%)	1076(40%)	493(19%)	131(5%)	45(2%)	25
Crude Oil(NYM)	86G-95V	2773	1347(49%)	31(1%)	823(30%)	1118(40%)	550(20%)	222(8%)	29(1%)	26
Heating Oil(NYM)	86G-95V	2744	1306(48%)	2(0%)	1144(42%)	1023(37%)	422(15%)	108(4%)	38(1%)	24
Natural Gas(NYM)	92G-95V	1184	585(49%)	16(1%)	292(25%)	452(38%)	262(22%)	119(10%)	43(4%)	27
Coffee "C"(CSCE)	86H-95U	2646	1234(47%)	6(0%)	912(34%)	1012(38%)	436(16%)	210(8%)	66(2%)	25
Cocoa(CSCE)	86H-95U	2641	1267(48%)	36(1%)	965(37%)	1102(42%)	387(15%)	146(6%)	5(0%)	24
Sugar #11(CSCE)	86H-95V	2680	1265(47%)	21(1%)	726(27%)	1073(40%)	568(21%)	204(8%)	88(3%)	27
Orange Juice(CTN)	86F-95U	2705	1246(46%)	43(2%)	736(27%)	926(34%)	547(20%)	276(10%)	116(4%)	28
Wheat(CBT)	86H-95U	2671	1305(49%)	12(0%)	934(35%)	894(33%)	597(22%)	207(8%)	27(1%)	25
Corn(CBT)	86H-95U	2671	1301(49%)	42(2%)	942(35%)	974(36%)	421(16%)	223(8%)	57(2%)	25
Soybeans(CBT)	86F-95U	2734	1236(45%)	15(1%)	1061(39%)	1130(41%)	395(14%)	77(3%)	35(1%)	24
Cotton(CTN)	86H-95V	2676	1302(49%)	24(1%)	901(34%)	984(37%)	459(17%)	226(8%)	76(3%)	26
Live Cattle(CME)	86G-95V	2730	1370(50%)	18(1%)	1056(39%)	1057(39%)	379(14%)	145(5%)	35(1%)	24
Pork Bellies(CME)	86G-96G	2736	1344(49%)	3(0%)	949(35%)	1004(37%)	537(20%)	187(7%)	56(2%)	25
Live Hogs(CME)	86G-95V	2738	1310(48%)	10(0%)	856(31%)	1122(41%)	453(17%)	216(8%)	57(2%)	26

LBRMoore TRADING, INC.

Historical Oops Reports

Larry Williams coined the name "Oops" to describe the cases in which the market opened below the previous day's low and then rallied back above that low, thus closing the gap. (For the sell trades, the market must open above the previous day's high and then trade back down through that high.) This test assumes that a trade is entered at the previous day's low for the buy side and at the previous day's high for the sell side. We can then examine the data to see what would happen if we exited on the close of the day of entry, the next day's open or close, and the following day's close. Please remember that no slippage or commissions are factored into these statistics. Also, no money management stops are employed.

The data suggest that the optimal window for exit tends to be the next day's opening. We are not looking at this in terms of a mechanical trading strategy, but rather to see if this pattern has any long-term directional implications.

The next step in this study is to examine the effects of adding a trend filter with the condition that the ADX must be greater than 30. The slope of the ADX does not matter. These reports are titled "Historical Oops (ADX Gapper)." Again, it is important to examine the buy and sell side of a strategy separately to note any directional bias.

The first interesting observation is that the frequency of setups is reduced. It works out that the number of signals drops from an average of 45 per year to 8 per year per market. The overall profitability combining both sell and buy setups across all markets increases by 65 percent. (This is using the next morning's opening as an exit.) Finally, over half the markets show a significant improvement in the average net trade when the holding period is increased by one day. Of course, this should come as no surprise since a trend filter was included. In conclusion, this study is a useful exercise in attempting to quantify the degree of improvement an ADX filter adds to a strategy.

EXHIBIT A.12 Historical Oops Buy Report

Historical Oops Buy Report

Enter at: PD Low

Futures Data			Exit on Close				Exit on Next Open				Exit on Next Close				Exit on 2nd Close			
Future	Contracts	Total Days	Win(%)	Avg Net	Avg Profit	Avg Loss	Win(%)	Avg Net	Avg Profit	Avg Loss	Win(%)	Avg Net	Avg Profit	Avg Loss	Win(%)	Avg Net	Avg Profit	Avg Loss
SP	89H-95U	1732	69(70%)	354	1171	-1524	68(69%)	308	1343	-1961	55(56%)	229	1793	-1726	49(49%)	-62	2176	-2256
YX	89H-95U	1731	77(68%)	191	632	-753	72(64%)	159	690	-772	65(58%)	191	899	-767	61(54%)	130	1190	-1114
USAM	89H-95U	1724	85(63%)	87	360	-376	80(59%)	94	457	-433	76(56%)	52	575	-622	83(61%)	98	731	-913
ED	89H-95U	1731	63(61%)	29	91	-68	65(63%)	26	108	-112	60(58%)	35	151	-127	64(62%)	47	189	-186
SF	89H-95U	1731	123(58%)	27	342	-403	115(54%)	55	540	-514	104(49%)	2	643	-610	101(47%)	21	957	-824
DM	89H-95U	1731	126(56%)	24	287	-313	126(56%)	22	396	-458	125(56%)	-10	427	-562	115(51%)	-41	610	-728
BP	89H-95U	1731	109(51%)	49	378	-296	114(54%)	32	509	-517	107(50%)	-43	573	-665	116(54%)	63	854	-883
JY	89H-95U	1730	104(46%)	-39	321	-341	120(53%)	-37	489	-621	115(50%)	-33	579	-655	115(50%)	-21	780	-835
GC	89G-95V	1757	126(56%)	15	124	-126	113(50%)	-3	172	-181	120(54%)	2	210	-239	121(54%)	27	291	-284
SI	89H-95U	1732	133(62%)	53	215	-214	118(55%)	38	252	-226	118(55%)	43	319	-297	122(57%)	56	397	-397
HG	89H-95U	1732	123(52%)	23	213	-184	115(49%)	1	273	-257	122(52%)	-5	284	-315	126(53%)	12	403	-436
CL	89G-95V	1775	117(59%)	66	250	-205	120(61%)	49	277	-306	122(62%)	82	346	-349	117(59%)	92	470	-460
HO	89G-95V	1771	124(53%)	16	287	-288	132(56%)	-5	301	-401	121(52%)	-32	375	-468	118(50%)	-5	544	-563
NG	92G-95V	984	93(54%)	56	308	-243	81(47%)	-16	356	-352	88(51%)	52	503	-426	87(51%)	31	629	-587
KC	89H-95U	1725	131(56%)	114	610	-516	127(54%)	86	651	-584	132(56%)	-14	659	-885	118(50%)	-34	965	-1051
CC	89H-95U	1726	136(53%)	21	138	-109	126(49%)	4	161	-146	154(60%)	38	212	-220	138(53%)	14	280	-292
SB	89H-95V	1784	142(63%)	41	161	-160	130(57%)	33	191	-179	131(58%)	37	233	-230	143(63%)	64	281	-305
JO	89F-95U	1753	114(57%)	48	207	-165	108(54%)	51	278	-219	113(57%)	70	364	-315	105(53%)	64	455	-373
W	89H-95U	1737	84(57%)	28	133	-112	85(58%)	36	161	-134	86(59%)	25	202	-226	81(55%)	50	299	-255
C	89H-95U	1737	94(56%)	15	83	-72	98(58%)	28	107	-82	106(63%)	41	134	-118	103(61%)	63	192	-142
S	89F-95U	1772	95(58%)	62	227	-161	92(56%)	49	284	-247	88(53%)	38	337	-304	90(55%)	71	487	-428
CT	89H-95V	1749	127(56%)	80	325	-238	132(59%)	87	402	-360	142(63%)	124	495	-511	132(59%)	165	677	-562
LC	89G-95V	1775	69(52%)	14	145	-129	68(52%)	15	165	-143	76(58%)	57	242	-195	75(57%)	90	334	-231
PB	89G-96G	1875	97(56%)	40	255	-239	99(58%)	46	278	-269	93(54%)	63	416	-353	94(55%)	33	499	-528
LH	89G-95V	1780	89(58%)	34	145	-118	88(57%)	29	168	-156	97(63%)	63	232	-224	87(56%)	69	323	-261

EXHIBIT A.13 Historical Oops Sell Report

Historical Oops Sell Report

Enter at: PD High

Futures Data			Exit on Close				Exit on Next Open				Exit on Next Close				Exit on 2nd Close			
Future	Contracts	Total Days	Win(%)	Avg Net	Avg Profit	Avg Loss	Win(%)	Avg Net	Avg Profit	Avg Loss	Win(%)	Avg Net	Avg Profit	Avg Loss	Win(%)	Avg Net	Avg Profit	Avg Loss
SP	89H-95U	1732	85(52%)	51	922	-911	86(53%)	119	1083	-972	78(48%)	-2	1598	-1488	70(43%)	-335	1840	-1990
YX	89H-95U	1731	66(53%)	47	440	-400	72(58%)	138	549	-430	62(50%)	50	777	-676	55(44%)	-141	955	-1014
USAM	89H-95U	1724	99(51%)	-45	328	-430	100(51%)	-30	413	-497	91(47%)	-53	567	-596	94(48%)	-32	744	-755
ED	89H-95U	1731	60(50%)	0	71	-72	59(49%)	-15	90	-117	54(45%)	-25	133	-154	58(48%)	-39	171	-235
SF	89H-95U	1731	101(50%)	-42	381	-474	95(48%)	-3	535	-491	84(42%)	-109	718	-708	88(44%)	-157	887	-977
DM	89H-95U	1731	104(49%)	-21	299	-333	106(50%)	-1	393	-399	96(45%)	-98	472	-575	99(47%)	-121	637	-791
BP	89H-95U	1731	100(50%)	-10	367	-379	98(49%)	40	589	-477	93(46%)	-73	661	-699	96(48%)	-60	884	-915
JY	89H-95U	1730	91(47%)	-2	342	-305	111(57%)	109	556	-490	108(56%)	99	627	-564	103(53%)	35	869	-910
GC	89G-95V	1757	103(58%)	5	122	-157	100(56%)	45	213	-173	89(50%)	8	228	-214	103(58%)	50	318	-324
SI	89H-95U	1732	66(62%)	58	195	-169	73(69%)	98	239	-215	61(58%)	61	277	-231	58(55%)	102	398	-257
HG	89H-95U	1732	99(68%)	69	181	-171	90(62%)	101	319	-255	85(59%)	21	360	-461	72(50%)	8	502	-480
CL	89G-95V	1775	115(62%)	68	213	-170	118(64%)	54	264	-314	95(51%)	-3	344	-368	88(48%)	-35	469	-492
HO	89G-95V	1771	86(61%)	92	263	-180	90(64%)	82	326	-357	87(62%)	108	452	-458	79(56%)	95	722	-717
NG	92G-95V	984	45(60%)	147	383	-207	46(61%)	201	495	-265	44(59%)	147	585	-475	44(59%)	205	708	-509
KC	89H-95U	1725	96(68%)	249	579	-456	96(68%)	296	798	-776	86(61%)	195	963	-1008	88(62%)	312	1228	-1209
CC	89H-95U	1726	78(67%)	54	145	-128	73(62%)	68	188	-130	79(68%)	80	219	-207	72(62%)	124	345	-230
SB	89H-95V	1784	59(56%)	39	154	-104	65(61%)	55	192	-163	68(64%)	60	243	-267	57(54%)	33	341	-326
JO	89F-95U	1753	81(49%)	-10	188	-203	94(57%)	15	230	-274	84(51%)	-2	283	-301	86(52%)	-10	333	-389
W	89H-95U	1737	72(53%)	1	120	-136	73(54%)	14	149	-145	72(53%)	11	189	-192	76(56%)	23	243	-260
C	89H-95U	1737	77(56%)	11	76	-70	82(59%)	27	108	-90	78(57%)	18	131	-129	78(57%)	45	186	-139
S	89F-95U	1772	68(61%)	60	203	-161	65(58%)	82	275	-184	64(57%)	81	349	-278	59(53%)	93	502	-363
CT	89H-95U	1749	95(57%)	43	308	-302	99(59%)	88	403	-363	90(54%)	86	579	-483	95(57%)	68	638	-673
LC	89G-95V	1775	76(57%)	36	148	-112	70(52%)	22	150	-119	72(54%)	28	215	-190	68(51%)	22	268	-231
PB	89G-96G	1875	92(56%)	20	286	-315	98(59%)	19	320	-422	95(58%)	49	430	-467	100(61%)	62	504	-618
LH	89G-95V	1780	73(55%)	22	138	-122	77(58%)	37	165	-144	81(61%)	67	229	-191	82(62%)	83	287	-251

EXHIBIT A.14 Historical Oops (ADX Gapper) Buy Report

Historical Oops (ADX Gapper) Buy Report

Enter at: PD Low—Filters: Only ADX(12)>30 & w/ADX(28) trend

Futures Data			Exit on Close				Exit on Next Open				Exit on Next Close				Exit on 2nd Close			
Future	Contracts	Total Days	Win(%)	Avg Net	Avg Profit	Avg Loss	Win(%)	Avg Net	Avg Profit	Avg Loss	Win(%)	Avg Net	Avg Profit	Avg Loss	Win(%)	Avg Net	Avg Profit	Avg Loss
SP	89H-95U	1732	9(69%)	237	803	-1038	8(62%)	525	1534	-1090	7(54%)	310	1829	-1463	6(46%)	485	3075	-1736
YX	89H-95U	1731	12(60%)	-18	412	-663	11(55%)	19	539	-617	11(55%)	214	893	-617	11(55%)	426	1473	-853
USAM	89H-95U	1724	23(59%)	104	408	-332	24(62%)	137	488	-425	22(56%)	129	635	-526	21(54%)	18	714	-795
ED	89H-95U	1731	19(51%)	29	101	-47	24(65%)	42	117	-95	24(65%)	70	145	-68	29(78%)	119	199	-169
SF	89H-95U	1731	25(62%)	9	335	-534	23(57%)	68	603	-657	16(40%)	-142	773	-752	20(50%)	-88	1015	-1190
DM	89H-95U	1731	25(52%)	-55	262	-399	25(52%)	-50	445	-588	24(50%)	-146	401	-692	20(42%)	-225	669	-864
BP	89H-95U	1731	20(53%)	71	404	-299	23(61%)	103	534	-558	20(53%)	13	701	-752	21(55%)	298	1158	-764
JY	89H-95U	1730	17(42%)	-163	427	-600	17(42%)	-224	673	-887	16(40%)	-297	737	-986	16(40%)	-418	953	-1332
GC	89G-95V	1757	21(64%)	10	117	-178	17(52%)	0	222	-236	18(55%)	-25	306	-423	18(55%)	25	400	-425
SI	89H-95U	1732	17(63%)	73	241	-213	16(59%)	87	323	-257	14(52%)	-37	340	-443	16(59%)	44	468	-572
HG	89H-95U	1732	24(57%)	39	238	-226	19(45%)	19	379	-278	25(60%)	-10	272	-426	26(62%)	102	511	-561
CL	89G-95V	1775	30(67%)	116	327	-306	30(67%)	107	324	-326	33(73%)	258	441	-248	28(62%)	351	725	-266
HO	89G-95V	1771	29(66%)	120	359	-343	29(66%)	23	353	-613	25(57%)	0	467	-615	25(57%)	197	733	-510
NG	92G-95V	984	26(70%)	218	409	-234	25(68%)	198	485	-400	25(68%)	302	645	-413	24(65%)	360	875	-592
KC	89H-95U	1725	21(55%)	-53	810	-1119	18(47%)	-102	971	-1068	18(47%)	-482	930	-1752	16(42%)	-357	1952	-2037
CC	89H-95U	1726	16(55%)	60	219	-135	16(55%)	53	220	-152	17(59%)	84	301	-222	16(55%)	41	337	-323
SB	89H-95V	1784	31(62%)	63	193	-147	31(62%)	56	205	-186	27(54%)	61	281	-198	26(52%)	3	325	-345
JO	89F-95U	1753	19(63%)	138	353	-234	20(67%)	171	418	-322	20(67%)	273	601	-382	21(70%)	358	635	-288
W	89H-95U	1737	15(75%)	102	165	-85	15(75%)	122	199	-110	11(55%)	39	288	-265	11(55%)	51	401	-376
C	89H-95U	1737	15(62%)	55	116	-46	16(67%)	93	173	-67	20(83%)	138	190	-122	19(79%)	177	251	-105
S	89F-95U	1772	7(70%)	152	252	-79	7(70%)	-64	291	-892	6(60%)	-251	238	-984	4(40%)	-321	272	-717
CT	89H-95V	1749	29(63%)	194	439	-224	29(63%)	207	556	-388	32(70%)	224	625	-690	31(67%)	268	774	-778
LC	89G-95V	1775	18(55%)	31	140	-99	20(61%)	34	155	-153	23(70%)	117	252	-194	22(67%)	159	329	-180
PB	89G-96G	1875	14(50%)	51	366	-265	15(54%)	31	367	-356	21(75%)	180	442	-607	18(64%)	63	427	-592
LH	89G-95V	1780	15(47%)	20	232	-167	19(59%)	9	215	-293	20(62%)	39	261	-332	19(59%)	96	419	-375

EXHIBIT A.15 Historical Oops (ADX Gapper) Sell Report

Historical Oops (ADX Gapper) Sell Report

LBRMoore TRADING, INC.

Enter at: PD High—Filters: Only ADX(12)>30 & w/ ADX(28) trend

Future	Futures Data Contracts	Total Days	Exit on Close Win(%)	Avg Net	Avg Profit	Avg Loss	Exit on Next Open Win(%)	Avg Net	Avg Profit	Avg Loss	Exit on Next Close Win(%)	Avg Net	Avg Profit	Avg Loss	Exit on 2nd Close Win(%)	Avg Net	Avg Profit	Avg Loss
SP	89H-95U	1732	11(69%)	292	832	-895	8(50%)	408	1431	-616	9(56%)	378	1825	-1482	8(50%)	136	2116	-1844
YX	89H-95U	1731	7(70%)	170	282	-92	5(50%)	280	675	-115	6(60%)	312	954	-650	5(50%)	112	1190	-965
USAM	89H-95U	1724	9(47%)	-89	295	-434	10(53%)	-20	397	-483	10(53%)	-12	394	-462	10(53%)	35	534	-521
ED	89H-95U	1731	8(53%)	18	103	-80	9(60%)	18	96	-100	6(40%)	11	192	-110	9(60%)	-4	154	-242
SF	89H-95U	1731	11(48%)	-100	376	-536	14(61%)	-41	423	-764	13(57%)	-145	533	-1026	12(52%)	53	881	-851
DM	89H-95U	1731	14(47%)	23	363	-275	19(63%)	190	578	-480	20(67%)	158	490	-506	19(63%)	53	653	-984
BP	89H-95U	1731	18(58%)	121	539	-457	19(61%)	392	937	-472	18(58%)	176	874	-790	20(65%)	456	1163	-830
JY	89H-95U	1730	13(38%)	-104	375	-400	21(62%)	231	674	-486	20(59%)	173	702	-583	20(59%)	405	1275	-838
GC	89G-95V	1757	19(61%)	22	124	-140	15(48%)	12	151	-119	12(39%)	-68	239	-262	14(45%)	-81	300	-395
SI	89H-95U	1732	10(77%)	107	194	-183	11(85%)	139	209	-243	8(62%)	132	291	-123	9(69%)	244	484	-295
HG	89H-95U	1732	10(59%)	65	196	-121	12(71%)	108	223	-167	12(71%)	111	285	-308	11(65%)	84	319	-348
CL	89G-95V	1775	22(76%)	120	182	-76	20(69%)	127	256	-160	16(55%)	53	327	-285	18(62%)	137	404	-302
HO	89G-95V	1771	6(60%)	86	239	-145	7(70%)	89	256	-298	8(80%)	98	227	-418	8(80%)	187	307	-292
NG	92G-95V	984	8(73%)	177	353	-290	9(82%)	257	444	-585	7(64%)	103	576	-725	7(64%)	181	699	-725
KC	89H-95U	1725	17(65%)	102	425	-509	14(54%)	213	745	-408	12(46%)	58	799	-578	14(54%)	413	1107	-397
CC	89H-95U	1726	16(64%)	19	103	-130	15(60%)	29	153	-157	18(72%)	50	165	-244	15(60%)	88	268	-181
SB	89H-95V	1784	9(50%)	-17	141	-175	10(56%)	-7	146	-197	11(61%)	-30	168	-341	10(56%)	-27	216	-332
JO	89F-95U	1753	12(41%)	-98	173	-290	14(48%)	-73	266	-390	10(34%)	-103	248	-288	16(55%)	-74	265	-491
W	89H-95U	1737	13(54%)	4	100	-110	13(54%)	20	128	-107	13(54%)	-30	147	-240	15(62%)	-78	141	-443
C	89H-95U	1737	9(36%)	-24	82	-83	13(52%)	-2	103	-115	12(48%)	-17	131	-154	15(60%)	16	132	-160
S	89F-95U	1772	10(53%)	62	270	-169	11(58%)	28	217	-231	11(58%)	-3	234	-328	6(32%)	-166	300	-381
CT	89H-95V	1749	9(56%)	109	349	-200	13(81%)	288	422	-288	12(75%)	429	750	-536	10(62%)	307	896	-674
LC	89G-95V	1775	7(64%)	59	149	-98	6(55%)	70	207	-95	3(27%)	-30	541	-245	3(27%)	-116	343	-289
PB	89G-96G	1875	15(60%)	35	276	-328	14(56%)	22	331	-371	14(56%)	-32	307	-464	13(52%)	-34	357	-457
LH	89G-95V	1780	13(54%)	12	96	-87	13(54%)	37	158	-107	17(71%)	86	192	-171	13(54%)	22	263	-262

ADX Buy and Sell Reports

This study tests buying (or selling) a close that is less than (or greater than) the close of two days ago during periods in which the ADX is above 30 and **rising**. Trades are taken only in the direction of the trend. No protective stops are used, nor are commissions and slippage factored in. We are merely testing to see what sort of an edge the ADX might offer for use as a filter in further system development. Two powerful statistics jump out at us! The first is the overwhelming positive expectation that the ADX filter provides. This is clearly an excellent departure from which to pursue the development of trading strategies. The second interesting statistic is the decrease in frequency of setups and the drop-off in the win/loss ratio on the sell-side. This might be due to the tendency of markets to go down faster than they go up. It might also suggest that very few retracement/entry opportunities exist at the beginning of a sharp decline. The times that the market allows us to sell a close higher than the close two days ago in a downtrending market, tend to occur late in the move. Thus, there is a drop-off in the profitability on the sell-side.

EXHIBIT A.16 Historical Fresh ADX Buy Report

LBRMoore TRADING, INC.

Historical Fresh ADX Buy Report

Enter on: Close

Futures Data			Exit on Next Close				Exit on 2nd Close				Exit on 3rd Close				Exit on 4th Close			
Future	Contracts	Total Days	Win(%)	Avg Net	Avg Profit	Avg Loss	Win(%)	Avg Net	Avg Profit	Avg Loss	Win(%)	Avg Net	Avg Profit	Avg Loss	Win(%)	Avg Net	Avg Profit	Avg Loss
SP	86H-95U	2500	30(49%)	110	1223	-968	31(51%)	48	1588	-1542	34(56%)	119	1501	-1620	37(61%)	354	1518	-1442
YX	86H-95U	2499	28(55%)	52	563	-570	28(55%)	-10	763	-951	28(55%)	39	916	-1029	28(55%)	180	979	-791
US	86H-95U	2498	52(50%)	-31	357	-426	60(58%)	95	627	-648	68(66%)	262	831	-845	67(65%)	395	980	-693
ED	86H-95U	2503	48(74%)	45	108	-132	45(69%)	67	174	-174	44(68%)	102	250	-210	47(72%)	134	289	-269
SF	86H-95U	2503	32(53%)	23	564	-596	29(48%)	121	951	-656	30(50%)	111	1075	-852	36(60%)	222	1105	-1103
DM	86H-95U	2503	43(64%)	51	345	-477	39(58%)	152	584	-450	41(61%)	182	650	-556	35(52%)	153	854	-614
BP	86H-95U	2503	28(56%)	126	629	-515	31(62%)	246	830	-706	29(58%)	250	934	-695	29(58%)	228	1040	-894
JY	86H-95U	2502	30(50%)	-146	461	-754	33(55%)	-19	675	-866	36(60%)	256	975	-823	41(68%)	608	1214	-701
GC	86G-95V	2528	28(60%)	40	329	-386	27(57%)	47	539	-617	24(51%)	96	793	-631	25(53%)	1	732	-828
SI	86H-95U	2501	18(50%)	-151	301	-603	16(44%)	-288	352	-800	16(44%)	-381	456	-1051	13(36%)	-460	681	-1105
HG	86H-95U	2501	26(60%)	163	503	-357	28(65%)	273	686	-498	25(58%)	371	1012	-519	24(56%)	459	1264	-557
CL	86G-95V	2562	22(47%)	-121	251	-449	28(60%)	19	320	-425	24(51%)	-17	473	-528	31(66%)	124	557	-714
HO	86G-95V	2554	17(71%)	-41	381	-1067	17(71%)	202	721	-1058	18(75%)	182	859	-1849	17(71%)	341	1027	-1326
NG	92G-95V	984	12(63%)	118	461	-470	13(68%)	267	614	-485	13(68%)	339	847	-760	13(68%)	461	1022	-753
KC	86H-95U	2493	21(50%)	296	1724	-1132	19(45%)	387	2623	-1460	23(55%)	556	3249	-2703	22(52%)	727	4306	-3211
CC	86H-95U	2490	17(46%)	-11	252	-234	19(51%)	-59	233	-367	17(46%)	2	415	-348	18(49%)	-11	431	-429
SB	86H-95U	2548	37(60%)	39	226	-237	39(63%)	76	344	-379	38(61%)	111	482	-478	38(61%)	83	478	-543
JO	86F-95U	2525	41(65%)	191	412	-220	46(73%)	341	599	-357	43(68%)	358	692	-360	44(70%)	424	774	-385
W	86H-95U	2509	34(55%)	43	236	-192	34(55%)	84	340	-225	28(45%)	-1	382	-316	33(53%)	4	320	-356
C	86H-95U	2509	22(54%)	9	118	-116	20(49%)	-9	182	-191	23(56%)	-17	210	-308	25(61%)	22	236	-313
S	86F-95U	2552	20(67%)	98	464	-634	16(53%)	94	704	-603	12(40%)	-77	1030	-815	12(40%)	-27	1264	-888
CT	86H-95U	2519	27(51%)	60	385	-278	34(64%)	221	623	-498	32(60%)	278	852	-597	36(68%)	315	825	-766
LC	86G-95V	2549	31(54%)	46	189	-126	35(61%)	71	247	-209	33(58%)	45	237	-219	29(51%)	62	351	-237
PB	86G-96G	2637	22(49%)	44	561	-450	28(62%)	71	551	-719	26(58%)	89	695	-740	23(51%)	-53	727	-868
LH	86G-95V	2557	30(51%)	33	250	-192	31(53%)	67	347	-244	33(56%)	90	387	-288	32(54%)	43	418	-402

EXHIBIT A.17 Historical Fresh ADX Sell Report

Historical Fresh ADX Sell Report

Enter on: Close

Futures Data			Exit on Next Close				Exit on 2nd Close				Exit on 3rd Close				Exit on 4th Close			
Future	Contracts	Total Days	Win(%)	Avg Net	Avg Profit	Avg Loss	Win(%)	Avg Net	Avg Profit	Avg Loss	Win(%)	Avg Net	Avg Profit	Avg Loss	Win(%)	Avg Net	Avg Profit	Avg Loss
SP	86H-95U	2500	15(44%)	-51	2277	-1889	17(50%)	10	2950	-2931	14(41%)	-18	3748	-2654	10(29%)	-252	5210	-2528
YX	86H-95U	2499	24(48%)	6	817	-742	21(42%)	-150	1362	-1246	16(32%)	-205	1995	-1240	14(28%)	-221	2398	-1239
US	86H-95U	2498	17(49%)	39	654	-542	17(49%)	113	857	-589	19(54%)	264	1036	-652	19(54%)	228	1120	-832
ED	86H-95U	2503	24(55%)	-85	125	-337	22(50%)	-94	193	-382	24(55%)	-78	243	-463	21(48%)	-61	326	-414
SF	86H-95U	2503	17(47%)	-82	363	-480	20(56%)	108	688	-616	18(50%)	276	1020	-467	23(64%)	514	1139	-591
DM	86H-95U	2503	15(43%)	-51	327	-334	18(51%)	73	699	-590	19(54%)	209	843	-545	18(51%)	160	940	-666
BP	86H-95U	2503	14(56%)	-37	684	-955	16(64%)	288	1121	-1194	14(56%)	284	1461	-1215	13(52%)	231	1754	-1419
JY	86H-95U	2502	10(37%)	-162	436	-515	11(41%)	-173	530	-656	10(37%)	-115	856	-687	10(37%)	-196	847	-810
GC	86G-95V	2528	30(50%)	-14	206	-234	23(38%)	2	500	-307	20(33%)	-34	536	-318	24(40%)	-65	441	-401
SI	86H-95U	2501	16(39%)	-112	154	-282	16(39%)	-175	226	-432	15(37%)	-230	250	-507	15(37%)	-260	286	-574
HG	86H-95U	2501	29(60%)	25	183	-216	29(60%)	43	259	-288	24(50%)	45	418	-328	28(58%)	95	429	-374
CL	86G-95V	2562	15(37%)	-74	335	-310	20(49%)	-124	353	-579	19(46%)	-84	386	-489	19(46%)	-124	438	-610
HO	86G-95V	2554	18(49%)	-68	356	-470	19(51%)	-51	481	-613	18(49%)	24	648	-567	23(62%)	153	716	-773
NG	92G-95V	984	12(86%)	116	252	-700	9(64%)	222	571	-406	9(64%)	232	820	-826	9(64%)	227	823	-846
KC	86H-95U	2493	39(51%)	-64	486	-643	37(49%)	-14	837	-821	31(41%)	109	1623	-935	39(51%)	225	1524	-1144
CC	86H-95U	2490	23(41%)	18	246	-140	29(52%)	52	270	-183	33(59%)	75	292	-238	31(55%)	31	295	-298
SB	86H-95V	2548	32(52%)	15	180	-166	27(44%)	-15	238	-215	33(54%)	23	289	-292	32(52%)	8	314	-330
JO	86F-95U	2525	27(47%)	-24	230	-253	28(49%)	-9	368	-373	27(47%)	-54	454	-511	24(42%)	-95	555	-567
W	86H-95U	2509	22(49%)	-18	138	-167	23(51%)	-5	167	-185	21(47%)	-15	201	-204	20(44%)	-21	232	-223
C	86H-95U	2509	28(51%)	-1	97	-103	32(58%)	19	152	-165	30(55%)	15	189	-194	29(53%)	29	227	-192
S	86F-95U	2552	15(39%)	-69	223	-260	14(37%)	-198	224	-445	11(29%)	-264	170	-442	9(24%)	-303	258	-478
CT	86H-95V	2519	24(56%)	36	369	-384	21(49%)	-16	659	-661	18(42%)	-22	963	-732	17(40%)	-54	1029	-762
LC	86G-95V	2549	15(48%)	22	274	-214	14(45%)	-18	349	-320	11(35%)	-145	422	-456	11(35%)	-206	428	-555
PB	86G-96G	2637	31(55%)	50	279	-234	31(55%)	7	371	-444	30(54%)	14	480	-524	36(64%)	175	608	-604
LH	86G-95V	2557	15(41%)	-21	195	-169	19(51%)	-35	179	-261	15(41%)	-104	245	-342	16(43%)	-123	274	-426

Gap Failure Reports

This report examines the setup where the market opens above the previous day's high and closes in the lower 50 percent of its range (indicating a sell setup), and the cases where the market opens below the previous day's low and closes in the upper 50 percent of its range (indicating a buy setup). The gap does not necessarily have to be filled as it does in the "Oops" strategy. We are testing the difference between the close of the entry bar and the next day's opening price. The trade opens in our favor almost 60 percent of the time. The average net profit also shows a positive expectation across almost all markets on both the buy and the sell side. It is interesting to note that despite an upward directional bias to the financial markets over the last 10 years, this strategy has better statistics on the sell-side! We conclude that there is a definite tendency for markets to follow through on the next day's opening after a Gap Failure setup.

EXHIBIT A.18 Historical Gap Failure Buy 50% Report

LBRMoore TRADING, INC.
Historical Gap Failure Buy 50% Report

Enter on: Close

Futures Data				Exit on Next Open		
Future	Contracts	Total Days	Win(%)	Avg Net	Avg Profit	Avg Loss
SP	86H-95U	2500	70(62%)	96	370	-349
YX	86H-95U	2499	69(54%)	12	224	-235
US	86H-95U	2498	109(64%)	69	262	-275
ED	86H-95U	2503	99(64%)	37	94	-65
SF	86H-95U	2503	125(54%)	71	367	-271
DM	86H-95U	2503	136(55%)	32	250	-231
BP	86H-95U	2503	123(53%)	11	306	-323
JY	86H-95U	2502	130(50%)	-1	347	-355
GC	86G-95V	2528	139(56%)	6	103	-115
SI	86H-95U	2501	110(52%)	-12	91	-126
HG	86H-95U	2501	113(55%)	-4	135	-172
CL	86G-95V	2562	135(63%)	23	137	-173
HO	86G-95V	2560	127(60%)	-3	162	-254
NG	92G-95V	984	53(50%)	-36	108	-184
KC	86H-95U	2493	112(52%)	-8	314	-356
CC	86H-95U	2490	96(44%)	-13	94	-96
SB	86H-95V	2548	90(43%)	-13	90	-92
JO	86F-95U	2525	110(62%)	24	108	-113
W	86H-95U	2509	92(70%)	31	63	-43
C	86H-95U	2509	113(72%)	31	62	-47
S	86F-95U	2552	102(60%)	5	109	-149
CT	86H-95V	2519	125(62%)	30	157	-174
LC	86G-95V	2549	60(46%)	-2	77	-69
PB	86G-96G	2644	73(55%)	7	121	-132
LH	86G-95V	2557	87(55%)	4	64	-68

EXHIBIT A.19 Historical Gap Failure Sell 50% Report

LBRMoore TRADING, INC.
Historical Gap Failure Sell 50% Report

Enter on: Close

Futures Data				Exit on Next Open		
Future	Contracts	Total Days	Win(%)	Avg Net	Avg Profit	Avg Loss
SP	86H-95U	2500	72(62%)	84	386	-401
YX	86H-95U	2499	72(61%)	61	236	-212
US	86H-95U	2498	111(57%)	50	243	-209
ED	86H-95U	2503	88(53%)	-13	48	-83
SF	86H-95U	2503	114(54%)	39	354	-335
DM	86H-95U	2503	110(52%)	8	249	-255
BP	86H-95U	2503	108(53%)	46	361	-315
JY	86H-95U	2502	125(53%)	34	391	-364
GC	86G-95V	2528	126(62%)	35	146	-148
SI	86H-95U	2501	80(65%)	79	209	-159
HG	86H-95U	2501	90(54%)	29	193	-164
CL	86G-95V	2562	139(61%)	22	135	-156
HO	86G-95V	2560	115(57%)	-17	175	-276
NG	92G-95V	984	35(67%)	88	186	-112
KC	86H-95U	2493	98(61%)	56	519	-677
CC	86H-95U	2490	80(56%)	12	96	-94
SB	86H-95U	2548	79(63%)	46	116	-71
JO	86F-95U	2525	89(64%)	46	122	-88
W	86H-95U	2509	82(72%)	22	55	-64
C	86H-95U	2509	112(71%)	17	50	-63
S	86F-95U	2552	83(61%)	42	150	-128
CT	86H-95V	2519	97(64%)	82	208	-144
LC	86G-95V	2549	54(45%)	-21	60	-88
PB	86G-96G	2651	79(53%)	2	120	-132
LH	86G-95V	2557	79(63%)	7	67	-96

2-Period Channel Breakout

This study examines the consequences of buying the highest high of the last two bars and then exiting and going short when the market breaks below the lowest low of the last two bars. This is called a 2-period channel breakout system. As you can see, there is a positive expectation across just about all markets. This is represented by the column which shows the Net Average for each trade.

This study is not intended to be an entry technique or an exit strategy! It merely supplies some quantitative evidence to support the theory that it is not wise to be long when the market takes out a two-day low, nor short when the market takes out the two-day high! I (Linda) have on occasion used it as a catastrophic stop. I have also used a 2-period channel as a way to trail a stop in a trending market.

EXHIBIT A.20 Historical Channel (2-Period High/Low) Report)

Historical Channel (CH:2:2:HL) Stop & Reverse Report

Market	Contracts	Total Days	Long Trades	Long Win(%)	Long Average	Short Trades	Short Win(%)	Short Average	Net Trades	Net Win(%)	Net Average
SP	86H-95U	2500	351	151(43%)	$256	354	125(35%)	$-97	705	276(39%)	$79
YX	86H-95U	2499	348	154(44%)	$134	351	120(34%)	$-48	699	274(39%)	$43
USAM	86H-95U	2495	345	149(43%)	$125	336	130(39%)	$-46	681	279(41%)	$40
ED	86H-95U	2503	304	134(44%)	$76	303	118(39%)	$16	607	252(42%)	$46
SF	86H-95U	2503	351	143(41%)	$59	352	122(35%)	$-57	703	265(38%)	$1
DM	86H-95U	2503	349	140(40%)	$77	348	116(33%)	$-33	697	256(37%)	$22
BP	86H-95U	2503	330	140(42%)	$198	331	120(36%)	$85	661	260(39%)	$141
JY	86H-95U	2502	338	131(39%)	$144	339	116(34%)	$8	677	247(36%)	$76
GC	86G-95V	2528	349	118(34%)	$-27	351	141(40%)	$27	700	259(37%)	$0
SI	86H-95U	2501	334	102(31%)	$7	346	132(38%)	$82	680	234(34%)	$45
HG	86H-95U	2501	353	156(44%)	$93	344	123(36%)	$-19	697	279(40%)	$38
CL	86G-95V	2562	387	148(38%)	$10	375	125(33%)	$-6	762	273(36%)	$2
HO	86G-95V	2560	366	161(44%)	$90	350	141(40%)	$65	716	302(42%)	$78
NG	92G-95V	984	134	63(47%)	$85	129	52(40%)	$88	263	115(44%)	$86
KC	86H-95U	2493	355	123(35%)	$-48	349	151(43%)	$117	704	274(39%)	$34
CC	86H-95U	2490	362	114(31%)	$-43	361	143(40%)	$37	723	257(36%)	$-3
SB	86H-95V	2548	340	137(40%)	$29	340	115(34%)	$-1	680	252(37%)	$14
JO	86F-95U	2525	353	136(39%)	$27	353	124(35%)	$11	706	260(37%)	$19
W	86H-95U	2509	340	139(41%)	$18	351	129(37%)	$0	691	268(39%)	$9
C	86H-95U	2509	317	124(39%)	$29	323	154(48%)	$57	640	278(43%)	$43
S	86F-95U	2552	346	124(36%)	$3	365	141(39%)	$43	711	265(37%)	$24
CT	86H-95V	2519	355	151(43%)	$64	355	115(32%)	$-74	710	266(37%)	$-5
LC	86G-95V	2549	330	151(46%)	$82	323	124(38%)	$18	653	275(42%)	$50
PB	86G-96G	2639	341	124(36%)	$25	348	149(43%)	$88	689	273(40%)	$57
LH	86G-95V	2557	363	134(37%)	$31	374	118(32%)	$-32	737	252(34%)	$-1

Samples of Daily Worksheets

Date:_____   LBRGroup Order Sheet

	CRUDE	HEAT OIL	SFRANC	MARK	POUND	YEN	GOLD	SILVER	COPPER
O									
H									
L									

	GAS	COFFEE	COCOA	SUGAR	WHEAT	CORN	BEANS	CATTLE	HOGS
O									
H									
L									

	BONDS	S&P			POSITIONS				
O									
H									
L									

WINNERS READILY ADMIT ERRORS   **CORRECT MISTAKES IMMEDIATELY**

LBRGroup Trade Sheet

DATE	B/S	✔	MARKET	ENTRY	✔	EXIT	SIZE & NOTES

TRADEMARKS

The following are trademarks held by Connors, Bassett & Associates:
- TURTLE SOUP
- TURTLE SOUP plus ONE
- 80-20's

The following are trademarks held by Linda Bradford Raschke:
- MOMENTUM PINBALL
- LBR/RSI
- ANTI

RESEARCH SERVICES, SOFTWARE, AND CHARTING SERVICES

Resources:

Aspen Research Group, Ltd.
710 Cooper Avenue, Suite 300
P.O. Box 1370
Glenwood Spring, Colorado 81602
(800) 359-1121

Moore Research Center
85180 Lorane Highway
Eugene, Oregon 97405
(800) 927-7259

LBRMoore Trading, Inc.
321 West 13th Avenue
Eugene, Oregon 97401
(503) 344-9448

Bill Wolfe
910 Stuart Avenue
Mamaraneck, New York 10543

SMR (Security Market Research)
P.O. Box 7476
Boulder, Colorado 80306
(303) 494-8035

Insight Trading Software
Barry Vaniel
25382 Village Road
Dana Point, California 92629
(714) 240-0990

Other Products from
M. GORDON PUBLISHING GROUP

Street Smarts Indicators for Omega Trade Station™ and SuperCharts

We have created an add-on module that allows you to identify the setups from *Street Smarts* on your version of Omega Trade Station™ and SuperCharts. This software alerts you to daily and intraday signals, plots the indicators, and also provides you with a daily printout for each day's entry points.

PRICE: $150.00

TRADING CONNORS VIX REVERSALS

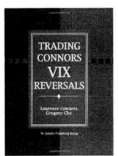

LAURENCE CONNORS AND GREG CHE

Here is Larry Connors' First Published Research In Over Three Years!

In this just-released guide, you will learn 10 strategies to trade the VIX. Five of these strategies have never been published before! Connors VIX Reversals have correctly predicted the direction of the S&Ps over the past 8 1/2 years approximately 65% of the time within a 2-to-3-day period. Some of these indicators have correctly predicted the market direction nearly 70% of the time!

Within this book you will learn ...

- **The new CVR strategies taught in his manual are even better than the originals. As powerful as the original signals were, these new signals have pushed the envelope ... with some performing with nearly 70% accuracy.**
- **Trading market sentiment? As you know, the VIX is one of the best ways to measure market sentiment. But, no one has ever measured and quantified the VIX the way Connors and Che do.**
- **Trade mechanically and objectively. $100,000 grew to over $1.9 million in 8 1/2 years if CVR signals were traded mechanically.**

SPECIAL BONUS! Included with this manual is Connors' 30 minute audio tape in which he further explains to you how to best trade the CVR signals.

Through both back testing and actual use in trading, the Connors VIX Reversals have proven to be one of the premier market timing tools for serious S&P traders, options traders, and stock traders. Put this new research to use in your trading today!

P.S. Don't forget that when you order today, you will also receive Larry's 30 minute audio tape that helps explain in more detail how best to use the CVR signals effectively!

98 PAGES SPIRAL BOUND $100.00

THE ANSWERS: The TradingMarkets.com Trading Advisor

EDDIE KWONG, EDITOR

What is the one thing that is worth far more than money? It's the unique and powerful knowledge that only a few traders possess that has allowed them to accumulate incalculable success. What if you could get the answers, directly from top traders, to your most important trading questions?

Now, in *The Answers*, you get direct and invaluable answers to some of the most essential trading questions ever asked—from real traders in real trading situations. Trading giants such as Kevin Haggerty, Gary Kaltbaum, Jeff Cooper, Dave Landry, and others, fully explore and give in-depth answers using the powerful knowledge that has kept them successful. In this dynamic new trading manual, you will learn: how to use Futures to gauge the strength or weakness of stocks, what the telltale signs of a major trend change are, how to distinguish between a minor pullback within a powerful trend and a major change in the trend, the best way to profit from false breakouts, and much, much more. In this extraordinary collection of Q&A's, you will benefit, first hand, from the strategies and techniques these traders have used over the years for their continued success in an ever-changing marketplace.

This book is a must read for every trader who wants to be successful!

212 PAGES HARD COVER $39.95

TO ORDER GO TO: www.mgordonpub.com **OR CALL:** 1-800-797-2584 or 1-213-955-5777 (outside the U.S.)

CONNORS ON ADVANCED TRADING STRATEGIES
31 Chapters on Beating the Markets

LAURENCE A. CONNORS

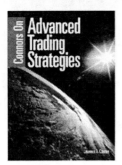

Written by Larry Connors, this new book is broken into seven sections; S&P and stock market timing, volatility, new patterns, equities, day-trading, options, and more advanced trading strategies and concepts. Thirty-one chapters of in-depth knowledge to bring you up to the same level of trading as the professionals.

Among the strategies you will learn are:

- **Connors VIX Reversals I, II and III (Chapter 2)**—Three of the most powerful strategies ever revealed. You will learn how the CBOE OEX Volatility Index (VIX) pinpoints short-term highs and lows in the S&Ps and the stock market. The average profit/trade for this method is among the highest Larry has ever released.
- **The 15 Minute ADX Breakout Method (Chapter 20)**—Especially for daytraders! This dynamic method teaches you how to specifically trade the most explosive futures and stocks every day! This strategy alone is worth the price of the book.
- **Options (Section 5)**—Four chapters and numerous in-depth strategies for trading options. You will learn the strategies used by the best Market Makers and a small handful of professionals to consistently capture options gains!
- **Crash, Burn, and Profit (Chapter 11)**—Huge profits occur when stocks implode. During a recent 12-month period, the Crash, Burn and Profit strategy shorted Centennial Technologies at 49 1/8; six weeks later it was at 2 1/2! It shorted Diana Corp. at 67 3/8; a few months later it collapsed to 4 3/8! It recently shorted Fine Host at 35; eight weeks later the stock was halted from trading at 10! This strategy will be an even bigger bonanza for you in a bear market.
- **Advanced Volatility Strategies (Section 2)**—Numerous, never-before revealed strategies and concepts using volatility to identify markets immediately before they explode.
- and much, much more!

259 PAGES HARD COVER $150.00

Dave Landry On Swing Trading:
A Momentum-Based Approach to Capturing Short-Term Market Moves

DAVE LANDRY

No time to daytrade? Intermediate-term and long-term trading not enough? Then swing trading is for you. Now, David Landry, Director of Trading Research for TradingMarkets.com, has put his entire swing trading methodology into one book to teach you how to trade successfully every day. Software Add-on Modules Available Now!

Dave Landry on Swing Trading takes you from his daily routine to the exact methods he uses day-in and day-out in his own analysis and trading. More than a dozen momentum-based strategies that pinpoint opportunities based on pullbacks and capitalize on false market moves. He also teaches you how to use volatility to select the right stocks and low-risk/high-reward setups. This is a complete manual on swing trading which includes everything the beginner and intermediate trader needs to get started trading quickly.

The following sections are included in his book to help you improve your trading results:

- **Trend Qualifiers**—Learn how to precisely identify strongly trending stocks.
- **Stock Selection**—David Landry will show you how to narrow down your universe to pick the right stocks to trade.
- **Swing Trading Strategies**—More than a dozen swing trading strategies presented in an easy-to-read, easy-to-understand format. He provides you with the specific rules for entry and exit so you can start identifying the best trading opportunities immediately.

Landry also goes into great detail covering: Trading Master Section, Stock Market Timing, Money Management, Trader's Psychology . . . and much, much more!

220 PAGES HARDCOVER $100.00

TO ORDER GO TO: www.mgordonpub.com OR CALL: 1-800-797-2584 or 1-213-955-5777 (outside the U.S.)

There Is Only One Place In The World Where You Can Find Trading Information Like This Every Day!!!

The World's Largest Site For Traders

More Than 24,000 Pages of Trading Information!

Trading Commentary
Trading Courses
Trading Lessons
Trading Indicators
Trading Books
Trading Seminars

Free Trial

Daily
Equity Daytrading Opportunities
Best Institutional Trading Setups

From The Mind Of One Of Wall Street's Sharpest Traders... Before going off to manage his own money, **Kevin Haggerty** was the head of trading for Fidelity Capital Markets. Now see which stocks he is looking to pounce on today!

Three Times Weekly
Short-Term Options Opportunities
Find out what a *Market Wizard* is Trading

One Of The Best Options Traders In The World...Tony Saliba was featured in the classic trading book *Market Wizards* as one of the best options traders in the world. Here are the option positions he and his senior traders are looking at today.

Weekly
Intermediate-Term Stock Opportunities
Best RS and EPS Candidates To Trade

What Is One Of The World's Top Money Managers Focusing On Today? **Mark Boucher**, previously ranked #1 by Nelson's "World's Best Money Managers," gives you his list of the fastest-moving stocks to trade.

Daily
Daytrade The SPYs and QQQs
Proprietary Methodology

Daytrade the QQQs, SPYs and E-minis for a living...Don Miller trades these markets for a living and can teach you to do the same. Find out how to become a successful trader today!

Daily
Daytrading Opportunities
High-Yield Proprietary Daytrading Setups

This Man Achieved Returns of 428% in 1998, 668% in 1999, and 1132% in 2000... Trader **Dave Floyd's** proprietary strategies incorporate market dynamics, patterns, and momentum.

Daily
Short-Term Trading Opportunities
Thoroughly Researched Swing Trading Setups

Are You A Short-Term Trader? Every night **Dave Landry**, director of research for TradingMarkets.com and author of *Dave Landry on Swing Trading*, shows you the best stock and futures setups for the next day's trading.

Twice Weekly
Intermediate-Term Stock Opportunities
The Most Stringent Trading Criteria

For Intermediate-Term Traders... Not only has hedge fund manager **Tim Truebenbach** beat the S&P 500 for 7 straight years, but 3 of them were in the triple digits! Find out today the stocks which meet his strict fundamental and technical criteria.

FREE OFFER

Go to **www.TradingMarkets.com**
or
Call Toll-Free **1-888-484-8220 x1**
NOW for your FREE 7-day trial!

Past results are not indicative of future returns. There is a risk of loss in trading.

ABOUT THE AUTHORS

Laurence Connors is founder and CEO of TradingMarkets.com. Larry has nearly 20 years experience in the financial markets industry, having started his brokerage career in 1981 at Merrill Lynch and completing it in 1994 as a Vice President with Donaldson, Lufkin and Jenrette. In addition to building two financial markets information companies, Larry has also authored four top-selling books on trading, including *Connors on Advanced Trading Strategies, Street Smarts, Investment Secrets of a Hedge Fund Manager,* and *Trading Connors VIX Reversals.*

Linda Bradford Raschke is a registered Commodity Trading Advisor. She is president of LBRGroup Trading Co., a firm specializing in money management and commercial hedging, and LBRMoore Trading, Inc., a firm specializing in research and system development.

FREE REPORT
Maximize Your Trading Profits Immediately

David Landry, TradingMarkets.com Director of Research, has put together a set of simple money management rules to help all traders become more successful in his report *The True Secret to Trading Success: Simple Money Management Rules That Will Make You a More Profitable Trader!*

To obtain this report, send your request along with your name and address to:

M. Gordon Publishing Group, Inc.
445 S. Figueroa Street, Suite 2930
Los Angeles, CA 90071

Or

Fax your information to 213-955-4242.

Your report will be mailed immediately.

CPSIA information can be obtained
at www.ICGtesting.com
Printed in the USA
BVHW011442241021
619604BV00006B/3